186020

AF334082

AUTHORITIES

Surveys and Explorations of Capt. J. C. Fremont, T. Eng.rs up to 1846. ———— Surveys & Expl.ns of Capt. H. Stansbury & Lieut. G. W. Gunnison, T. Eng.rs to & at Great Salt Lake, 1850. ———— Surveys & Expl.ns of Gov. I. I. Stevens & his parties, in connection with a proposed R. Road to the Pacific, 1854. ———— Surveys & Expl.ns of Lieuts. R. S. Williamson & H. L. Abbot, T. Eng.rs in Oregon &c., for R. Road purposes, 1855. ———— Reconnoissances of Lieut. G. H. Mendell, T. Eng.rs thro' the Region between Ft. Hall & Ft. Boisée, Snake R., 1855. ———— Survey for a Military Road from Ft. Vancouver to Steilacoom, by Lieut. G. H. Derby, T. Eng.rs 1855. ———— Survey for a Military Road from Astoria to Salem, by Lt. Derby, 1856. ———— U. S. Coast Survey Maps &c. relative to the Coast of the Pacific, 1856. ———— Gen.l Land Office Sketch Maps of Washington & Oregon Territories, 1857. ———— Sketch of Roads &c. in vicinity of Great Salt Lake, by T. S. Lander, 1857. ———— Survey for a Waggon Road to the Pacific, along Humboldt River, &c. by F. A. Bishop under superint.t of J. Kirk, 1857. ———— Survey for a Military Road from Fort Steilacoom to Bellingham Bay, by Lt. G. H. Mendell, T. E. 1857.

The Roads and great travelled Routes are indicated thus ————
Other Routes followed by the various exploring parties are indic.d thus ————

DEPARTMENT OF OREGON
MAP
of the
STATE OF OREGON
and
WASHINGTON
TERRITORY
compiled in
THE BUREAU OF TOPOG.L ENG.RS
chiefly for military purposes
by order of
HON. JOHN. B. FLOYD SEC. OF WAR
1859

Pacific City
Cape Disappointment
Light Ho.
Pt. Adams
Cathlamet
Astoria
Young's R.
Tamantown
Rainier
SADDLE MT.
St. Helens
Cowlitz R.
Tillamook Head
Nehalem R.
False Tillamook
Tillamook R.
MOUNTAINS
Cape Lookout
Fort Yamhill
Yamhill
N. Fork
Tualatin
Hillsboro
Lafayette
Dayton
Champoeg
Fairfield
Fort Hoskins
Nechesne R.
S. Fork Yamhill R.
RIVER
Nekas R.
Dallas
SALEM
La Creole R.
La Kimute R.
WILLAMETTE
Cape Foulweather
Salitz R.
COAST
Mill Cr.
N. Fork
Santiam
Yaquina R.
Corvallis
Albany
S. Fork of San
Calapooia Cr.
Alseya R.
RANGE
Alseya Settl.
Cape Perpetua
Long Tom R.
Siuslau River
Eugene City
McK
CALLAPOOYA
Gardiner
Smith's River
Umpqua
Fort Umpqua
Umpqua Head

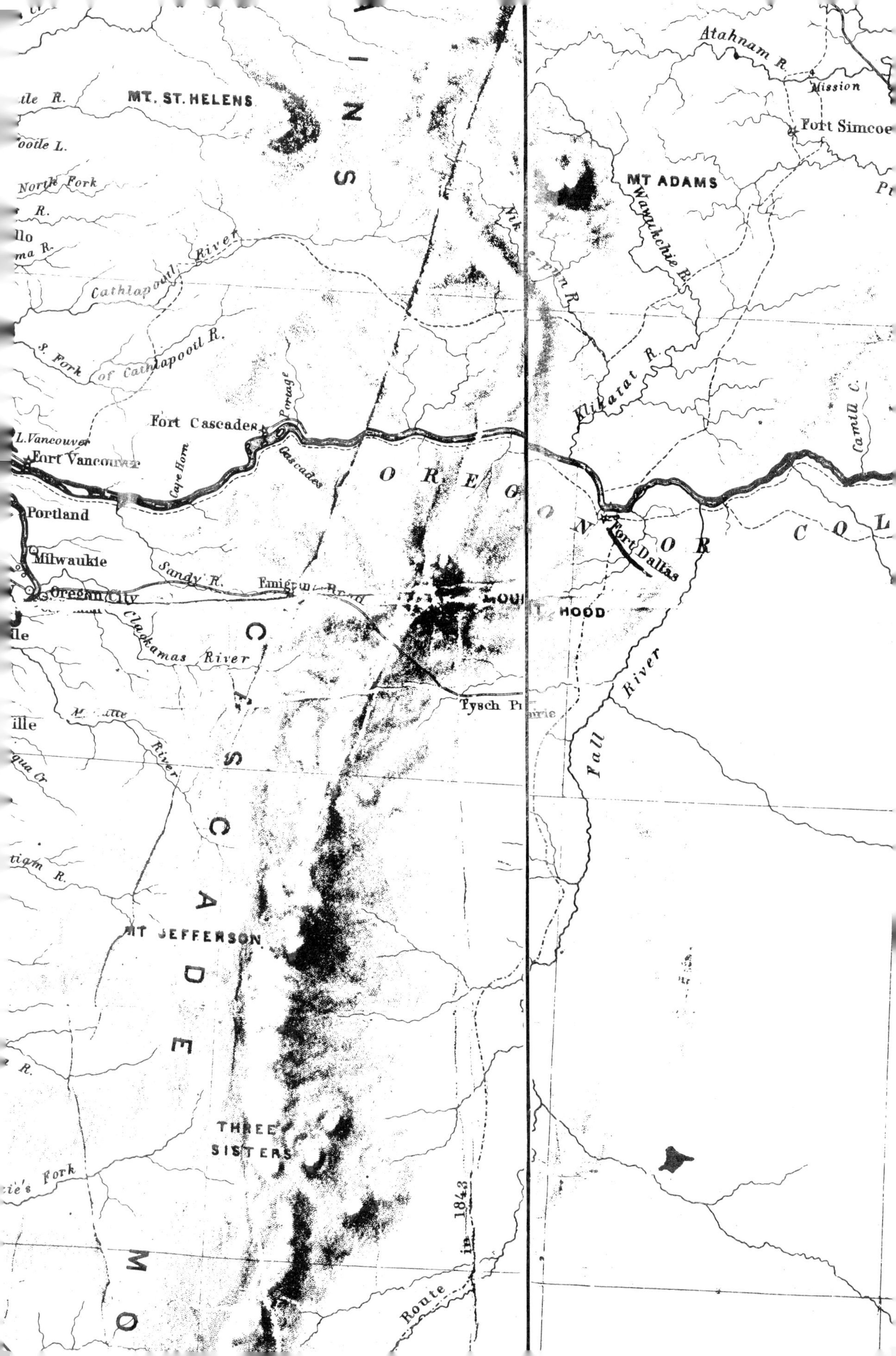

MT. ST. HELENS
Cathlapooil River
S. Fork of Cathlapooil R.
North Fork
Fort Cascades
Portage
Cape Horn
Cascades
L. Vancouver
Fort Vancouver
Portland
Milwaukie
Oregan City
Sandy R.
Emigrant Road
Clackamas River
MOUNT HOOD
Tysch Prairie
MT JEFFERSON
THREE SISTERS
C A S C A D E   M O
OREGON OR COL
Atahnam R.
Mission
Fort Simcoe
MT ADAMS
Wawukchie R.
Klikatat R.
Camill C.
Fort Dallas
Fall River
Route in 1843

INDIAN FIGHTING IN THE FIFTIES
IN OREGON AND WASHINGTON TERRITORIES

Eng.d by H.B. Hall's Sons. New York.

P. H. Sheridan
Brevet 2d Lieutenant
1st Regiment Infantry

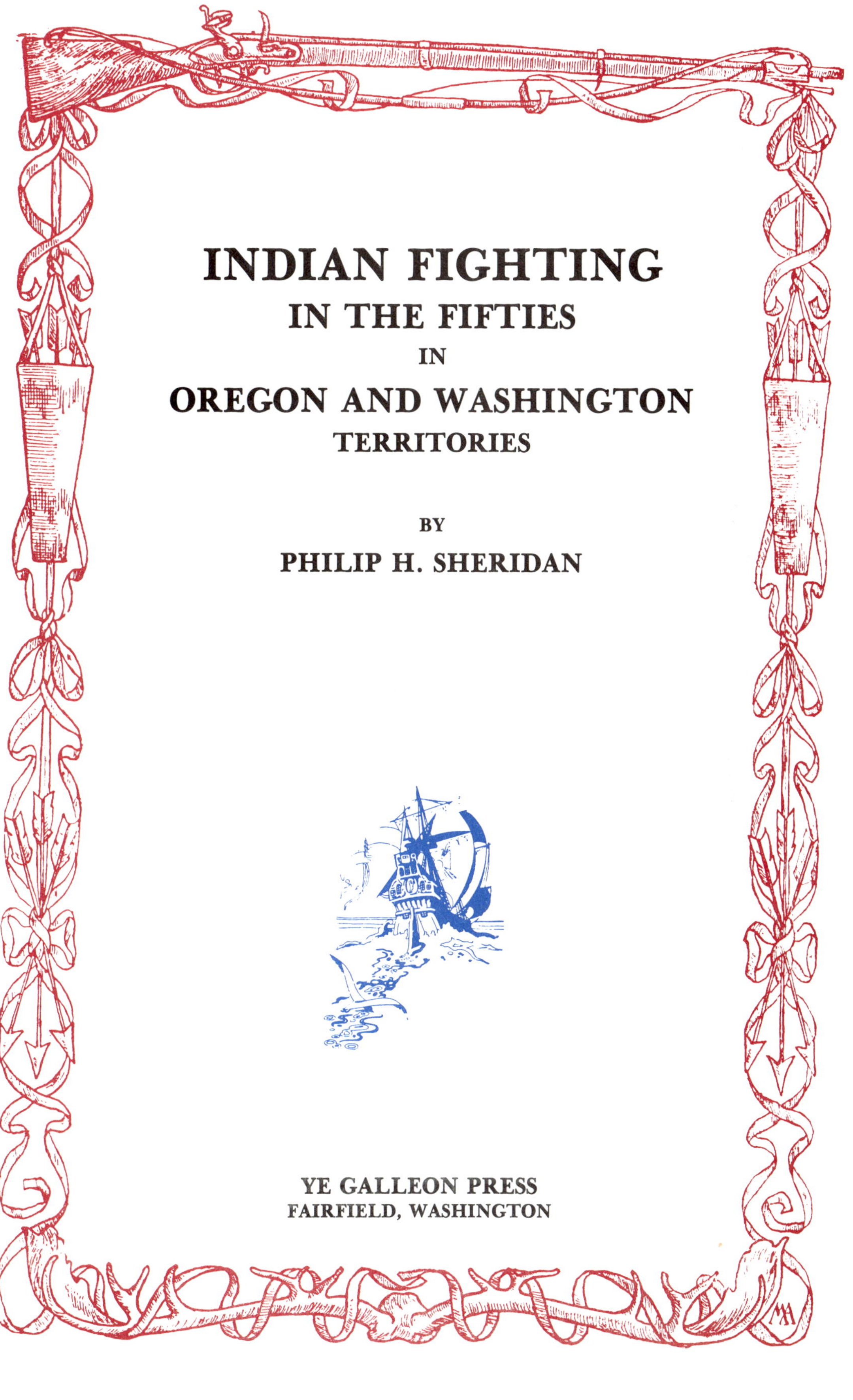

INDIAN FIGHTING
IN THE FIFTIES
IN
OREGON AND WASHINGTON
TERRITORIES

BY

PHILIP H. SHERIDAN

YE GALLEON PRESS
FAIRFIELD, WASHINGTON

Library of Congress Cataloging-in-Publication Data

Sheridan, Philip Henry, 1831-1888.
   Indian fighting in the fifties in Oregon and Washington Territories.

   Excerpts from Sheridan's personal memoirs.
   Includes index.
   1. Pacific Coast Indians, Wars with, 1847-1865 — Personal
narratives. 2. Sheridan, Philip Henry, 1831-1888. 3. Generals — United
States — Biography. 4. United States. Army — Biography. I. Title. II.
Title: Indian fighting in the 50s in Oregon and Washington Territories.

E83.84.S54   1987   973.7'3'0924   87-25411
ISBN 0-87770-438-4

PREFACE

HEN, YIELDING TO THE SOLICITATIONS OF MY FRIENDS, I finally decided to write these memoirs, the greatest difficulty which confronted me was that of recounting my share in the many notable events of the last three decades, in which I played a part, without entering too fully into the history of these years, and at the same time without giving to my own acts an unmerited prominence. To what extent I have overcome this difficulty I must leave the reader to judge.

In offering this record, penned by my own hand, of the events of my life, and of my participation in our great struggle for national existence, human liberty, and political equality, I make no pretension to literary merit; the importance of the subject-matter of my narrative is my only claim on the reader's attention.

Respectfully dedicating this work to my comrades in arms during the War of the Rebellion, I leave it as a heritage to my children, and as a source of information for the future historian.

P.H. SHERIDAN.

Nonquitt, Mass., August 2, 1888.

CHAPTER I.

Y PARENTS, JOHN AND MARY SHERIDAN, CAME TO America in 1830, having been induced by the representations of my father's uncle, Thomas Gainor, then living in Albany, N.Y., to try their fortunes in the New World. They were born and reared in the County Cavan, Ireland, where from early manhood my father had tilled a leasehold on the estate of Cherrymount; and the sale of this leasehold provided him with means to seek a new home across the sea. My parents were blood relations—cousins in the second degree—my mother, whose maiden name was Minor, having descended from a collateral branch of my father's family. Before leaving Ireland they had two children, and on the 6th of March, 1831, the year after their arrival in this country, I was born, in Albany, N.Y., the third child in a family which eventually increased to six—four boys and two girls.

The prospects for gaining a livelihood in Albany did not meet the expectations which my parents had been led to entertain, so in 1832 they removed to the West, to establish themselves in the village of Somerset, in Perry County, Ohio, which section, in the earliest days of the State, had been colonized from Pennsylvania and Maryland. At this period the great public works of the Northwest—the canals and macadamized roads, a result of clamor for internal improvements—were in course of construction, and my father turned his attention to them, believing that they offered opportunities for a successful occupation. Encouraged by a civil engineer named Bassett, who had taken a fancy to him, he put in bids for a small contract on the Cumberland Road, known as the "National Road," which was then being extended west from the Ohio River. A little success in this first enterprise led him to take up contracting as a business, which he followed on various canals and macadamized roads then building in different parts of the State of Ohio, with some good fortune for awhile, but in 1853 what little means he had saved were swallowed up in bankruptcy, caused by the failure of the Sciota and Hocking Valley Railroad Company, for which he was fulfilling a contract at the time, and this disaster left him finally only a small farm, just outside the village of Somerset, where he dwelt until his death in 1875.

My father's occupation kept him away from home much of the time during my boyhood, and as a consequence I grew up under the sole guidance and training of my mother, whose excellent common sense and clear discernment in every way fitted her for such maternal duties. When old enough I was sent to the village school, which was taught by an old-time Irish "master"—one of those itinerant dominies of the early frontier—who, holding that to spare the rod was to spoil the child, if unable to detect the real culprit when any offense had been committed, would consistently apply the switch to the whole school without discrimination. It must be conceded that by this means he never failed to catch the guilty mischief-maker. The school-year was divided into terms of three months, the teacher being paid in each term a certain sum—three dollars, I think, for each pupil—and having an additional perquisite in the privilege of boarding around at his option in the different families to which his scholars belonged. This feature was more than acceptable to the parents at times, for how else could they so thoroughly learn all the neighborhood gossip? But the pupils were in almost unanimous opposition, because Mr. McNanly's unheralded advent at any one's house resulted frequently in the discovery that some favorite child had been playing "hookey," which means (I will say to the uninitiated, if any such there be) absenting one's self from school without permission, to go on a fishing or a swimming frolic. Such at least was my experience more than once, for Mr. McNanly particularly favored my mother's house, because of a former acquaintanceship in Ireland, and many a time a comparison of notes proved that I had been in the woods with two playfellows, named Binckly and Greiner, when the master thought I was home, ill, and my mother, that I was at school, deeply immersed in study. However, with these and other delinquencies not uncommon among boys, I learned at McNanly's school, and a little later, under a pedagogue named Thorn, a smattering of geography and history, and explored the mysteries of Pike's Arithmetic and Bullions' English Grammar, about as far as I could be carried up to the age of fourteen. This was all the education then bestowed upon me, and this—with the exception of progressing in some of these branches by voluntary study, and by practical application in others, supplemented by a few months of preparation after receiving my appointment as a cadet—was the extent of my learning on entering the Military Academy.

When about fourteen years old I began to do something for myself; Mr. John Talbot, who kept a country store in the village, employing me to deal out sugar, coffee, and calico to his customers at the munificent salary of twenty-four dollars a year. After I had gained a twelvemonths' experience with Mr. Talbot my services began to be sought by others, and a Mr. David Whitehead secured them by the offer of sixty dollars a year—Talbot refusing to increase my pay, but not objecting to my advancement. A few months later, before my year was up, another chance to increase my salary came about; Mr. Henry Dittoe, the enterprising man of the village, offering me one hundred and twenty dollars a year to take a position in the dry goods store of Fink & Dittoe. I laid the matter before Mr. Whitehead, and he frankly advised me to accept, though he cautioned me that I might regret it, adding that he was afraid Henry (referring to Mr. Dittoe) "Had too many irons in the fire." His warning in regard to the enterprising merchant proved a prophecy, for "too many irons in the fire" brought about Mr. Dittoe's bankruptcy, although this misfortune did not befall him till long after I had left his service. I am glad to say, however, that his failure was an exceptionally honest one, and due more to the fact that he was in advance of his surroundings than to any other cause.

I remained with Fink & Dittoe until I entered the Military Academy, principally in charge of the book-keeping, which was no small work for one of my years, considering that in those days the entire business of country stores in the West was conducted on the credit system; the customers, being mostly farmers, never expecting to pay till the product of their farms could be brought to market; and even then usually squared the book-accounts by notes of hand, that were often slow of collection.

From the time I ceased to attend school my employment had necessitated, to a certain degree, the application of what I had learned there, and this practical instruction I reinforced somewhat by doing considerable reading in a general way, until ultimately I became quite a local authority in history, being frequently chosen as arbiter in discussions and disputes that arose in the store. The Mexican War, then going on, furnished, of course, a never-ending theme for controversy, and although I was too young to enter the military service when volunteers were mustering in our section, yet the stirring events of the times so much impressed and absorbed me that my sole wish was to become a soldier, and my highest aspiration to go to West Point as a Cadet from my Congressional district. My chances for this seemed very remote, however, till one day an opportunity was thrown in my way by the boy who then held the place failing to pass his examination. When I learned that by this occurrence a vacancy existed, I wrote to our representative in Congress, the Hon. Thomas Ritchey, and asked him for the appointment, reminding him that we had often met in Fink & Dittoe's store, and that therefore he must know something of my qualifications. He responded promptly by enclosing my warrant for the class of 1848; so, notwithstanding the many romances that have been published about the matter, to Mr. Ritchey, and to him alone, is due all the credit—if my career justifies that term—of putting me in the United States Army.

At once I set about preparing for the examination which precedes admission to the Military Academy, studying zealously under the direction of Mr. William Clark; my old teachers, McNanly and Thorn, having disappeared from Somerset and sought new fields of usefulness. The intervening months passed rapidly away, and I fear that I did not make much progress, yet I thought I should be able to pass the preliminary examination. That which was to follow worried me more and gave me many sleepless nights; but these would have been less in number, I fully believe, had it not been for one specification of my outfit which the circular that accompanied my appointment demanded. This requirement was a pair of "Monroe shoes." Now, out in Ohio, what "Monroe shoes" were was a mystery—not a shoe-maker in my section having so much as an inkling of the construction of the perplexing things, until finally my eldest brother brought an idea of them from Baltimore, when it was found that they were a familiar pattern under another name.

At length the time for my departure came, and I set out for West Point, going by way of Cleveland and across Lake Erie to Buffalo. On the steamer I fell in with another appointee *en route* to the academy, David S. Stanley, also from Ohio; and when our acquaintanceship had ripened somewhat, and we had begun to repose confidence in each other, I found out that he had no "Monroe shoes," so I deemed myself just that much ahead of my companion, although my shoes might not conform exactly to the regulations in Eastern style and finish.

At Buffalo Stanley and I separated, he going by the Erie Canal and I by the railroad, since I wanted to gain time on account of commands to stop in Albany to see my father's uncle. Here I spent a few days, till Stanley reached Albany, when we journeyed together down the river to West Point. The examination began a few days after our arrival, and I soon found myself admitted to the Corps of Cadets, to date from July 1, 1848, in a class composed of sixty-three members, many of whom—for example, Stanley, Slocum, Woods, Kautz, and Crook—became prominent generals in later years, and commanded divisions, corps, and armies in the war of rebellion.

Quickly following my admission I was broken in by a course of hazing, with many of the approved methods that the Cadets had handed down from year to year since the Academy was founded; still, I escaped excessive persecution, although there were in my day many occurrences so extreme as to call forth condemnation and an endeavor to suppress the senseless custom, which an improved civilization has now about eradicated, not only at West Point, but at other colleges.

Although I had met the Academic board and come off with fair success, yet I knew so little of Algebra or any of the higher branches of mathematics that during my first six months at the Academy I was discouraged by many misgivings as to the future, for I speedily learned that at the January examination the class would have to stand a test much severer than that which had been applied to it on entering. I resolved to try hard, however, and, besides, good fortune gave me for a room-mate a Cadet whose education was more advanced than mine, and whose studious habits and willingness to aid others benefited me immensely. This room-mate was Henry W. Slocum, since so signally distinguished in both military and civil capacities as to win for his name a proud place in the annals of his country. After taps—that is, when by the regulations of the Academy all the lights were supposed to be extinguished, and everybody in bed—Slocum and I would hang a blanket over the one window of our room and continue our studies—he guiding me around scores of stumbling-block in Algebra and elucidating many knotty points in other branches of the course with which I was unfamiliar. On account of this association I went up before the Board in January with less uneasiness than otherwise would have been the case, and passed the examination fairly well. When it was over, a self-confidence in my capacity was established that had not existed hitherto, and at each succeeding examination I gained a little in order of merit till my furlough summer came round—that is, when I was half through the four-year course.

My furlough in July and August, 1850, was spent at my home in Ohio, with the exception of a visit or two to other Cadets on furlough in the State, and at the close of my leave I returned to the Academy in the full expectation of graduating with my class in 1852.

A quarrel of a belligerent character in September, 1851, with Cadet William R. Terrill, put an end to this anticipation, however, and threw me back into the class which graduated in 1853. Terrill was a Cadet Sergeant, and, while my company was forming for parade, having given me an order, in what I considered an improper tone, to "dress" in a certain direction, when I believed I was accurately dressed, I fancied I had a grievance, and made toward him with a lowered bayonet, but my better judgment recalled me before actual contact could take place. Of course Terrill reported me for this, and my ire was so inflamed by his action that when we next met I attacked him, and a fisticuff engagement in front of barracks followed, which was stopped by an officer appearing on the scene. Each of us handed in an explanation, but mine was unsatisfactory to the authorities, for I had to admit that I was the assaulting party, and the result was that I was suspended by the Secretary of War, Mr. Conrad, till August 28, 1852—the Superintendent of the Academy, Captain Brewerton, being induced to recommend this milder course, he said, by my previous good conduct. At the time I thought, of course, my suspension a very unfair punishment, that my conduct was justifiable and the authorities of the Academy all wrong, but riper experience has led me to a different conclusion, and as I look back, though the mortification I then endured was deep and trying, I am convinced that it was hardly as much as I deserved for such an outrageous breach of discipline.

There was no question as to Terrill's irritating tone, but in giving me the order he was prompted by the duty of his position as a file closer, and I was not the one to remedy the wrong which I conceived had been done me, and clearly not justifiable in assuming to correct him with my own hands. In 1862, when General Buell's army was assembling at Louisville, Terril was with it as a brigadier-general (for, although a Virginian, he had remained loyal), and I then took the initiative toward a renewal of our acquaintance. Our renewed friendship was not destined to be of long duration, I am sorry to say, for a few days later, in the battle of Perryville, while gallantly fighting for his country, poor Terrill was killed.

My suspension necessitated my leaving the Academy, and I returned home in the fall of 1851, much crestfallen. Fortunately, my good friend Henry Dittoe again gave me employment in keeping the books of his establishment, and this occupation of my time made the nine months which were to elapse before I could go back to West Point pass much more agreeably than they would have done had I been idle. In August, 1852, I joined the first class at the Academy in accordance with the order of the War Department, taking my place at the foot of the class and graduating with it the succeeding June, number thirty-four in a membership of fifty-two. At the head of this class graduated James B. McPherson, who was killed in the Atlanta campaign while commanding the Army of the Tennessee. It also contained such men as John M. Schofield, who commanded the Army of the Ohio; Joshua W. Sill, killed as a brigadier in the battle of Stone River; and many others who, in the war of the rebellion, on one side or the other, rose to prominence, General John B. Hood being the most distinguished member of the class among the Confederates.

At the close of the final examination I made no formal application for assignment to any particular arm of the service, for I knew that my standing would not entitle me to one of the existing vacancies, and that I should be obliged to take a place among the brevet second lieutenants. When the appointments were made I therefore found myself attached to the First Infantry, well pleased that I had surmounted all the difficulties that confront the student at our national school, and looking forward with pleasant anticipation to the life before me.

CHAPTER II.

ORDERED TO FORT DUNCAN, TEXAS—"NORTHERS"—SCOUTING DUTY
HUNTING—NEARLY CAUGHT BY THE INDIANS—A PRIMITIVE HABITATION
A BRAVE DRUMMER-BOY'S DEATH—A MEXICAN BALL..

ON THE 1ST DAY OF JULY, 1853, I WAS COMMISSIONED A brevet second lieutenant in the First Regiment of United States Infantry, then stationed in Texas. The company to which I was attached was quartered at Fort Duncan, a military post on the Rio Grande opposite the little town of Piedras Negras, on the boundary line between the United States and the Republic of Mexico.

After the usual leave of three months following graduation from the Military Academy I was assigned to temporary duty at the Newport Barracks, a recruiting station and rendezvous for the assignment of young officers preparatory to joining their regiments. Here I remained from September, 1853, to March, 1854, when I was ordered to join my company at Fort Duncan. To comply with this order I proceeded by steamboat down the Ohio and Mississippi rivers to New Orleans, thence by steamer across the Gulf of Mexico to Indianola, Tex., and after landing at that place, continued in a small schooner through what is called the inside channel on the Gulf coast to Corpus Christi, the headquarters of Brigadier-General Persifer F. Smith, who was commanding the Department of Texas. Here I met some of my old friends from the Military Academy, among them Lieutenant Alfred Gibbs, who in the last year of the rebellion commanded under me a brigade of cavalry, and Lieutenant Jerome Napoleon Bonaparte, of the Mounted Rifles, who resigned in 1854 to accept service in the French Imperial army, but to most of those about headquarters I was an entire stranger. Among the latter was Captain Stewart Van Vliet, of the Quartermaster's Department, now on the retired list. With him I soon came in frequent contact, and, by reason of his connection with the Quartermaster's Department, the kindly interest he took in forwarding my business inaugurated between us a lasting friendship.

A day or two after my arrival at Corpus Christi a train of Government wagons, loaded with subsistence stores and quartermaster's supplies, started for Laredo, a small town on the Rio Grande below Fort Duncan. There being no other means of reaching my station I put my small personal possessions, consisting of a trunk, mattress, two blankets, and a pillow into one of the heavily loaded wagons and proceeded to join it, sitting on the boxes or bags of coffee and sugar, as I might choose. The movement of the train was very slow, as the soil was soft on the newly made and sandy roads. We progressed but a few miles on our first day's journey, and in the evening parked our train at a point where there was no wood, a scant supply of water—and that of bad quality—but an abundance of grass. There being no comfortable place to sleep in any of the wagons, filled as they were to the bows with army supplies, I spread my blankets on the ground between the wheels of one of them, and awoke in the morning feeling as fresh and bright as would have been possible if all the comforts of civilization had been at my command.

It took our lumbering train many days to reach Laredo, a distance of about one hundred and sixty miles from Corpus Christi. Each march was but a repetition of the first day's journey, its monotony occasionally relieved, though, by the passage of immense flocks of ducks and geese, and the appearance at intervals of herds of deer, and sometimes droves of wild cattle, wild horses and mules. The bands of wild horses I noticed were sometimes led by mules, but generally by stallions with long wavy manes, and flowing tails which almost touched the ground.

We arrived at Laredo during one of those severe storms incident to that section, which are termed "Northers" from the fact that the north winds culminate occasionally in cold wind-storms, frequently preceded by heavy rains. Generally the blow lasts for three days, and the cold becomes intense and piercing. While the sudden depression of the temperature is most disagreeable, and often causes great suffering, it is claimed that these "Northers" make the climate more healthy and endurable. They occur from October to May, and in addition to the destruction which, through the sudden depression of the temperature, they bring on the herds in the interior, they are often of sufficient violence to greatly injure the harbors on the coast.

The post near Laredo was called Fort McIntosh, and at this period the troops stationed there consisted of eight companies of the Fifth Infantry and two of the First, one of the First Artillery, and three of the Mounted Rifles. Just before the "Norther" began these troops had completed a redoubt for the defense of the post, with the exception of the ditches, but as the parapet was built of sand—the only material about Laredo which could be obtained for its construction—the severity of the winds was too much for such a shifting substance, and the work was entirely blown away early in the storm.

I was pleasantly and hospitably welcomed by the officers at the post, all of whom were living in tents, with no furniture except a cot and trunk, and an improvised bed for a stranger, when one happened to come along. After I had been kindly taken in by one of the younger officers, I reported to the commanding officer, and was informed by him that he would direct the quarter-master to furnish me, as soon as convenient, with transportation to Fort Duncan, the station of my company.

In the course of a day or two, the quarter-master notified me that a Government six-mule wagon would be placed at my disposal to proceed to my destination. No better means offering, I concluded to set out in this conveyance, and, since it was also to carry a quantity of quarter-master's property for Fort Duncan, I managed to obtain room enough for my bed in the limited space between the bows and load, where I could rest tolerably well, and under cover at night, instead of sleeping on the ground under the wagon, as I had done on the road from Corpus Christi to Laredo.

I reached Fort Duncan in March, 1854, and was kindly received by the commanding officer of the regiment, Lieutenant-Colonel Thompson Morris, and by the captain of my company ("D"), Eugene E. McLean, and his charming wife, the daughter of General E.V. Sumner, who was already distinguished in our service, but much better known in after years in the operations of the Army of the Potomac, during its early campaigns in Virginia.

Shortly after joining company "D" I was sent out on scouting duty with another company of the regiment to Camp La Pena, about sixty or seventy miles east of Fort Duncan, in a section of country that had for some time past been subjected to raids by the Lipan and Comanche Indians. Our outpost at La Pena was intended as a protection against the predatory incursions of these savages, so almost constant scouting became a daily occupation. This enabled me soon to become familiar with and make maps of the surrounding country, and, through constant association with our Mexican guide, to pick up in a short time quite a smattering of the Spanish language, which was very useful to one serving on that frontier.

At that early day western Texas was literally filled with game, and the region in the immediate vicinity of La Pena contained its full proportion of deer, antelope, and wild turkeys. The temptation to hunt was therefore constantly before me, and a desire to indulge in this pastime, whenever free from the legitimate duty of the camp, soon took complete possession of me, so expeditions in pursuit of game were of frequent occurrence. In these expeditions I was always accompanied by a soldier named Frankman, belonging to "D" company, who was a fine sportsman, and a butcher by trade. In a short period I learned from Frankman how to approach and secure the different species of game, and also how to dress and care for it when killed. Almost every expedition we made was rewarded with a good supply of deer, antelope, and wild turkeys, and we furnished the command in camp with such abundance that it was relieved from the necessity of drawing its beef ration, much to the discomfiture of the disgruntled beef contractor.

The camp at La Pena was on sandy ground, unpleasant for men and animals, and by my advice it was moved to La Pendencia, not far from Lake Espantosa. Before removal from our old location, however, early one bright morning Frankman and I started on one of our customary expeditions, going down La Pena Creek to a small creek, at the head of which we had established a hunting rendezvous. After proceeding along the stream for three or four miles we saw a column of smoke on the prairie, and supposing it arose from a camp of Mexican rancheros catching wild horses or wild cattle, and even wild mules, which were very numerous in that section of the country along the Nueces River, we thought we would join the party and see how much success they were having, and observe the methods employed in this laborious and sometimes dangerous vocation. With this object in view, we continued on until we found it necessary to cross to the other side of the creek to reach the point indicated by the smoke. Just before reaching the crossing I discovered moccasin tracks near the water's edge, and realizing in an instant that the camp we were approaching might possibly be one of hostile Indians—all Indians in that country at that time were hostile—Frankman and I backed out silently, and made eager strides for La Pena, where we had scarcely arrived when Captain M.E. Van Buren, of the Mounted Rifle regiment, came in with a small command, and reported that he was out in pursuit of a band of Comanche Indians, which had been committing depredations up about Fort Clark, but that he had lost the trail. I immediately informed him of what had occurred to me during the morning, and that I could put him on the trail of the Indians he was desirous of punishing. We hurriedly supplied with rations his small command of thirteen men, and I then conducted him to the point where I had seen the smoke, and there we found signs indicating it to be the recently abandoned camp of the Indians he was pursuing, and we also noticed that prairie rats had formed the principal article of diet at the meal they had just completed. As they had gone, I could do no more than put him on the trail made in their departure, which was well marked; for Indians, when in small parties, and unless pressed, usually follow each other in single file. Captain Van Vuren followed the trail by Fort Ewell, and well down toward Corpus Christi, day and night, until the Indians, exhausted and used up, halted on an open plain, unsaddled their horses, mounted bareback, and offered battle. Their number was double that of Van Buren's detachment, but he attacked them fearlessly, and in the fight was mortally wounded by an arrow which entered his body in front, just above the sword belt, and came through the belt behind. The principal chief of the Indians was killed, and the rest fled. Captain Van Buren's men carried him to Corpus Christi, where in a few days he died.

After our removal to La Pendencia a similar pursuit of savages occurred, but with more fortunate results. Colonel John H. King, now on the retired list, then a captain in the First Infantry, came to our camp in pursuit of a marauding band of hostile Indians, and I was enabled to put him also on the trail. He soon overtook them, and killing two without loss to himself, the band disperssed like a flock of quail and left him nothing to follow. He returned to our camp shortly after, and the few friendly Indian scouts he had with him held a grand pow-wow and dance over the scalps of the fallen braves.

Around La Pendencia, as at La Pena, the country abounded in deer, antelope, wild turkeys, and quail, and we killed enough to supply abundantly the whole command with the meat portion of the ration. Some mornings Frankman and I would bring in as many as seven deer, and our hunting expeditions made me so familiar with the region between our camp and Fort Duncan, the headquarters of the regiment, that I was soon enabled to suggest a more direct route of communication than the circuitous one then traversed, and in a short time it was established.

Up to this time I had been on detached duty, but soon my own company was ordered into the field to occupy a position on Turkey Creek, about ten or twelve miles west of the Nueces River, on the road from San Antonio to Fort Duncan, and I was required to join the company. Here constant work and scouting were necessary, as our camp was specially located with reference to protecting from Indian raids the road running from San Antonio to Fort Duncan, and on to the interior of Mexico. In those days this road was the great line of travel, and Mexican caravans were frequently passing over it, to and fro, in such a disorganized condition as often to invite attack from marauding Comanches and Lipans. Our time, therefore, was incessantly occupied in scouting, but our labors were much lightened because they were directed with intelligence and justice by Captain McLean, whose agreeable manners and upright methods are still so impressed on my memory that to this day I look back upon my service with "D" Company of the First Infantry as among those events which I remember with most pleasure.

In this manner my first summer of active field duty passed rapidly away, and in the fall my company returned to Fort Duncan to go into winter quarters. These quarters, when constructed, consisted of "A" tents pitched under a shed improvised by the company. With only these accommodations I at first lived around as best I could until the command was quartered, and then, requesting a detail of wagons from the quarter-master, I went out some thirty miles to get poles to build a more comfortable habitation for myself. In a few days enough poles for the construction of a modest residence were secured and brought in, and then the building of my house began. First, the poles were cut the proper length, planted in a trench around four sides of a square of very small proportions, and secured at the top by string-pieces stretched from one angle to another, in which half-notches had been made at proper intervals to receive the uprights. The poles were then made rigid by strips nailed on half-way to the ground, giving the sides of the structure firmness, but the interstices were large and frequent; still, with the aid of some old condemned paulins obtained from the quartermaster, the walls were covered and the necessity for chinking obviated. This method of covering the holes in the side walls also possessed the advantage of permitting some little light to penetrate to the interior of the house, and avoided the necessity of constructing a window, for which, by the way, no glass could have been obtained. Next a good large fire-place and chimney were built in one corner by means of stones and mud, and then the roof was put on—a thatched one of prairie grass. The floor was dirt compactly tamped.

My furniture was very primitive: a chair or two, with about the same number of camp stools, a cot, and a rickety old bureau that I obtained in some way not now remembered. My washstand consisted of a board about three feet long, resting on legs formed by driving sticks into the ground until they held it at about the proper height from the floor. This washstand was the most expensive piece of furniture I owned, the board having cost me three dollars, and even then I obtained it as a favor, for lumber on the Rio Grande was so scarce in those days that to possess even the smallest quantity was to indulge in great luxury. Indeed, about all that reached the post was what came in the shape of bacon boxes, and the boards from these were reserved for coffins in which to bury our dead.

In this rude habitation I spent a happy winter, and was more comfortably off than many of the officers, who had built none, but lived in tents and took the chances of "Northers." During this period our food was principally the soldier's ration: flour, pickled pork, nasty bacon—cured in the dust of ground charcoal—and fresh beef, of which we had a plentiful supply, supplemented with game of various kinds. The sugar, coffee, and smaller parts of the ration were good, but we had no vegetables, and the few jars of preserves and some few vegetables kept by the sutler were too expensive to be indulged in. So during all the period I lived at Fort Duncan and its sub-camps, nearly sixteen months, fresh vegetables were pratically unobtainable. To prevent scurvy we used the juice of the maguey plant, called pulque, and to obtain a supply of this anti-scorbutic I was often detailed to march the company out about forty miles, cut the plant, load up two or three wagons with the stalks, and carry them to camp. Here the juice was extracted by a rude press, and put in bottles until it fermented and became worse in odor than sulphureted hydrogen. At reveille roll-call every morning this fermented liquor was dealt out to the company, and as it was my duty, in my capacity of subaltern, to attend these roll-calls, and see that the men took their ration of pulque, I always began the duty by drinking a cup of the repulsive stuff myself. Though hard to swallow, its well-known specific qualities in the prevention and cure of scurvy were familiar to all, so every man in the command gulped down his share notwithstanding its vile taste and odor.

Considering our isolation, the winter passed very pleasantly to us all. The post was a large one, its officers congenial, and we had many enjoyable occasions. Dances, races, and horseback riding filled in much of the time, and occasional raids from the Indians furnished more serious occupation in the way of a scout now and then. The proximity of the Indians at times rendered the surrounding country somewhat dangerous for individuals or small parties at a distance from the fort; but few thought the savages would come near, so many risks were doubtless run by various officers, who carried the familiar six-shooter as their only weapon while out horseback riding, until suddenly we were awakened to the dangers we had been incurring.

About mid-winter a party of hostile Lipans made a swoop around and skirting the garrison, killing a herder—a discharged drummer-boy—in sight of the flag-staff. Of course great excitement followed. Captain J.G. Walker, of the Mounted Rifles, immediately started with his company in pursuit of the Indians, and I was directed to accompany the command. Not far away we found the body of the boy filled with arrows, and near him the body of a fine looking young Indian, whom the lad had undoubtedly killed before he was himself overpowered. We were not a great distance behind the Indians when the boy's body was discovered, and having good trailers we gained on them rapidly, with the prospect of overhauling them, but as soon as they found we were getting near they headed for the Rio Grande, made the crossing to the opposite bank, and were in Mexico before we could overtake them. When on the other side of the boundary they grew very brave, daring us to come over to fight them, well aware all the time that the international line prevented us from continuing the pursuit. So we had to return to the post without reward for our exertion except the consciousness of having made the best effort we could to catch the murderers. That night, in company with Lieutenant Thomas G. Williams, I crossed over the river to the Mexican village of Piedras Negras, and on going to the house where a large *baille*, or dance, was going on we found among those present two of the Indians we had been chasing. As soon as they saw us they strung their bows for a fight, and we drew our six-shooters, but the Mexicans quickly closed in around the Indians and forced them out of the house—or rude *jackal*—where the "ball" was being held, and they escaped. We learned later something about the nature of the fight the drummer had made, and that his death had cost them dear, for, in addition to the Indian killed and lying by his side, he had mortally wounded another and seriously wounded a third, with the three shots that he had fired.

At this period I took up the notion of making a study of ornithology, incited to it possibly by the great number of bright-colored birds that made their winter homes along the Rio Grande, and I spent many a leisure hour in catching specimens by means of stick traps, with which I found little difficulty in securing almost every variety of the feathered tribes. I made my traps by placing four sticks of a length suited to the size desired to as to form a square, and building up on them in log-cabin fashion until the structure came almost to a point by contraction of the corners. Then the sticks were made secure, the trap placed at some secluded spot, and from the centre to the outside a trench was dug in the ground, and thinly covered when a depth had been obtained that would leave an aperture sufficiently large to admit the class of birds desired. Along this trench seeds and other food were scattered, which the birds soon discovered, and of course began to eat, unsuspectingly following the tempting bait through the gallery till they emerged from its farther end in the centre of the trap, where they contentedly fed till the food was all gone. Then the fact of imprisonment first presented itself, and they vainly endeavored to escape through the interstices of the cage, never once guided by their instinct to return to liberty through the route by which they had entered. Among the different kinds of birds captured in this way, mocking-birds, blue-bird, robins, meadow larks, quail, and plover were the most numerous. They seemed to have more voracious appetites than other varieties, or else they were more unwary, and consequently more easily caught. A change of station, however, put an end to my ornithological plans, and activities of other kinds prevented me from resuming them in after life.

There were quite a number of young officers at the post during the winter, and as our relations with the Mexican commandant at Piedras negras were most amicable, we were often invited to dances at his house. He and his hospitable wife and daughter drummed up the female portion of the elite of Piedras Negras and provided the house, which was the official as well as the personal residence of the commandant, while we—the young officers—furnished the music and such sweetmeats, candies, &c., for the *baille* as the country would afford.

We generally danced in a long hall on a hard dirt floor. The girls sat on one side of the hall, chaperoned by their mothers or some old duennas, and the men on the other. When the music struck up each man asked the lady whom his eyes had already selected to dance with him, and it was not etiquette for her to refuse—no engagements being allowed before the music began. When the dance, which was generally a long waltz, was over, he seated his partner, and then went to a little counter at the end of the room and bought his dulcinea a plate of the candies and sweetmeats provided. Sometimes she accepted them, but most generally pointed to her duenna or chaperon behind, who held up her apron and caught the refreshments as they were slid into it from the plate. The greatest decorum was maintained at these dances, primitively as they were conducted; and in a region so completely cut off from the world, their influence was undobtedly beneficial to a considerable degree in softening the rough edges in a half-breed population.

The inhabitants of this frontier of Mexico were strongly marked with Indian characteristics, particularly with those of the Comanche type, and as the wild Indian blood predominated, few of the physical traits of the Spaniard remained among them, and outlawry was common. The Spanish conquerors had left on the northern border only their graceful manners and their humility before the cross. The sign of Christinity was prominently placed at all important points on roads or trails, and especially where any one had been killed; and as the Comanche Indians, strong and warlike, had devastated northeastern Mexico in past years, all along the border, on both sides of the Rio Grande, the murderous effects of their raids were evidenced by numberless crosses. For more than a century forays had been made on the settlements and towns by these blood-thirsty savages, and, the Mexican Government being too weak to afford protection, property was destroyed, the women and children carried off or ravished, and the men compelled to look on in an agony of helplessness till relieved by death. During all this time, however, the forms and ceremonials of religion, and the polite manners received from the Spaniards, were retained, and reverence for the emblems of Christianity was always uppermost in the mind of even the most ignorant.

Fort Vancouver
COLUMBIA RIVER
PORTLAND
MT HOOD
WILLIAMETTE RIVER
RIVER
THREE SISTERS
DES CHUTES
COLUMBIA RIVER
KLAMATH RIVER
PIT RIVER
P.C. RIVER
FORT READING
LOWER
Mc CLOUD
LASSENS BUTTE
N
W E
S
Scale
10 0 10 20 30 40 50 miles
Lieut. Williamson's trail,
from Fort Reading Cal.
to Fort Vancouver W.T.

CHAPTER III.

IN NOVEMBER, 1854, I RECEIVED MY PROMOTION TO A second lieutenancy in the Fourth Infantry, which was stationed in California and oregon. In order to join my company at Fort Reading, California I had to go to New York as a starting-point, and on arrival there, was placed on duty, in May, 1855, in command of a detachment of recruits at Bedloe's Island, intended for assignment to the regiments on the Pacific coast. I think there were on the island (now occupied by the statue of Liberty Enlightening the World) about three hundred recruits. For a time I was the only officer with them, but shortly before we started for California, Lieutenant Francis H. Bates, of the Fourth Infantry, was placed in command. We embarked for the Pacific coast in July, 1855, and made the journey without incident *via* the Isthmus of Panama, in due time landing our men at Benecia Barracks, above San Francisco.

From this point I proceeded to join my company at Fort Reading, and on reaching that post, found orders directing me to relieve Lieutenant John B. Hood—afterward well known as a distinguished general in the Confederate service. Lieutenant Hood was in command of the personal mounted escort of Lieutenant R.S. Williamson, who was charged with the duty of making such explorations and surveys as would determine the practicability of connecting, by railroad, the Sacramento Valley in California with the Columbia

River in Oregon Territory, either through the Willamette Valley, or (if this route should prove to be impracticable) by the valley of the Des Chutes River near the foot-slopes of the Cascade chain. The survey was being made in accordance with an act of Congress, which provided both for ascertaining the most practicable and economical route for a railroad between the Mississippi River and the Pacific Ocean, and for military and geographical surveys west of the Mississippi River.

Fort Reading was the starting-point for this exploring expedition, and there I arrived some four or five days after the party under Lieutenant Williamson had begun its march. His personal escort numbered about sixty mounted men, made up of detachments from companies of the First Dragoons, under command of Lieutenant Hood, together with about one hundred men belonging to the Fourth Infantry and Third Artillery, commanded by Lieutenant Horatio Gates Gibson, the present colonel of the Third United States Artillery. Lieutenant George Crook — now major-general — was the quartermaster and commissary of subsistence of the expedition.

The commanding officer at Fort Reading seemed reluctant to let me go on to relieve Lieutenant Hood, as the country to be passed over was infested by the Pit River Indians, known to be hostile to white people and especially to small parties. I was very anxious to proceed, however, and willing to take chances; so consent being finally obtained, I started with a corporal and two mounted men, through a wild and uninhabited region, to overtake if possible Lieutenant Williamson. Being on horseback, and unencumbered by luggage of any kind except blankets and a little hard bread, coffee and smoking-tobacco, which were all carried on our riding animals, we were sanguine of succeeding, for we traversed in one day fully the distance made in three by Lieutenant Williamson's party on foot.

The first day we reached the base of Lassan's Butte, where I determined to spend the night near an isolated cabin, or dugout, that had been recently constructed by a hardy pioneer. The wind was blowing a disagreeable gale, which had begun early in the day. This made it desirable to locate our camp under the best cover we could find, and I spent some little time in looking about for a satisfactory place, but nothing better offered than a large fallen tree, which lay in such a direction that by encamping on its lee side we would be protected from the fury of the storm. This spot was therefore fixed upon, and preparation made for spending the night as comfortably as the circumstances would permit.

After we had unsaddled I visited the cabin to inquire in regard to the country ahead, and there found at first only a soldier of Williamson's party' later the proprietor of the ranch appeared. The soldier had been left behind by the surveying party on account of illness, with instructions to make his way back to Fort Reading as best he could when he recovered. His condition having greatly improved, however, since he had been left, he now begged me in beseeching terms to take him along with my party, which I finally consented to do, provided that if he became unable to keep up with me, and I should be obliged to abandon him, the responsibility would be his, not mine. This increased my number to five, and was quite a reinforcement should we run across any hostile Indians; but it was also certain to prove an embarrassment should the man again fall ill.

During the night, notwithstanding the continuance of the storm, I had a very sound and refreshing sleep behind the protecting log where we made our camp, and at daylight next morning we resumed our journey, fortified by a breakfast of coffee and hard bread. I skirted around the base of Lassan's Butte, thence down Hat Creek, all the time following the trail made by Lieutenant Williamson's party. About noon the soldier I had picked up at my first camp gave out, and could go no farther. As stipulated when I consented to take him along, I had the right to abandon him, but when it came to the test I could not make up my mind to do it. Finding a good place not far off the trail, one of my men volunteered to remain with him until he died; and we left them there, with a liberal supply of hard bread and coffee, believing that we would never again see the invalid. My reinforcement was already gone, and another man with it.

With my diminished party I resumed the trail and followed it until about 4 o'clock in the afternoon, when we heard the sound of voices, and the corporal, thinking we were approaching Lieutenant Williamson's party, was so overjoyed in anticipation of the junction, that he wanted to fire his musket as an expression of his delight. This I prevented his doing, however, and we continued cautiously and slowly on to develop the source of the sounds in front. We had not gone far before I discovered that the noise came from a band of Pit River Indians, who had struck the trail of the surveying expedition and were following it up, doubtless with evil intent. Dismounting from my horse I counted the moccasin tracks to ascertain the number of Indians, discovered it to be about thirty, and then followed on behind them cautiously, but with little difficulty, as appearances of speed on their part indicated that they wished to overtake Lieutenant Williamson's party, which made them less on the lookout than usual for any possible pursuers. After following the trail until nearly sundown, I considered it prudent to stop for the night, and drew off some little distance, where, concealed in a dense growth of timber, we made our camp.

As I had with me now only two men, I felt somewhat nervous, so I allowed no fires to be built, and in consequence our supper consisted of hard bread only. I passed an anxious night, but beyond our own solicitude there was nothing to disturb us, the Indians being too much interested in overtaking the party in front to seek for victims in the rear. After a hard-bread breakfast we started again on the trail, and had proceeded but a short distance when, hearing the voices of the Indians, we at once slackened our speed so as not to overtake them.

Most of the trail on which we traveled during the morning ran over an exceedingly rough lava formation—a spur of the lava beds often described during the Modoc war of 1873—so hard and flinty that Williamson's large command made little impression on its surface, leaving in fact, only indistinct traces of its line of march. By care and frequent examinations we managed to follow his route through without much delay, or discovery by the Indians, and about noon, owing to the termination of the lava formation, we descended into the valley of Hat Creek, a little below where it emerges from the second canon and above its confluence with Pit River. As soon as we reached the fertile soil of the valley, we found Williamson's trail well defined, deeply impressed in the soft loam, and coursing through wild-flowers and luxuriant grass which carpeted the ground on every hand.

When we struck this delightful locality we traveled with considerable speed, and after passing over hill and vale for some distance, the trail becoming more and more distinct all the time, I suddenly saw in front of me the Pit River Indians. This caused a halt, and having hurriedly re-capped our guns and six-shooters, thus preparing for the worst, I took a look at the band through my field-glass. They were a half-mile or more in our front and numbered about thirty individuals, armed with bows and arrows only. Observing us they made friendly demonstrations, but I had not implicit faith in a Pit River Indian at that period of the settlement of our country, and especially in that wild locality, so after a "council of war" with the corporal and man, I concluded to advance to a point about two hundred yards distant from the party, when, relying on the speed of our horses rather than on the peaceable intentions of the savages, I hoped to succeed in cutting around them and take the trail beyond. Being on foot they could not readily catch us, and inasmuch as their arrows were good for a range of only about sixty yards, I had no fear of any material damage on that score.

On reaching the place selected for our flank movement we made a dash to the left of the trail, through the widest part of the valley, and ran our horses swiftly by, but I noticed that the Indians did not seem to be disturbed by the manoeuvre and soon realized that this indifference was occasioned by the knowledge that we could not cross Hat Creek, a deep stream with vertical banks, too broad to be leaped by our horses. We were obliged, therefore, to halt, and the Indians again made demonstrations of friendship, some of them even getting into the stream to show that they were at the ford. Thus reassured, we regained our confidence and boldly crossed the river in the midst of them. After we had gained the bluff on the other side of the creek, I looked down into the valley of Pit River, and could plainly see the camp of the surveying party. Its proximity was the influence which had doubtless caused the peaceable conduct of the Indians. Probably the only thing that saved us was their ignorance of our being in the rear, until we stumbled on them almost within sight of the large party under Williamson.

The Pit River Indians were very hostile at that time, and for many succeeding years their treachery and cruelty brought misfortune and misery to the white settlers who ventured their lives in search of home and fortune in the wild and isolated section over which these savages roamed. Not long after Williamson's party passed through their country, the Government was compelled to send into it a considerable force for the purpose of keeping them under control. The outcome of this was a severe fight — resulting in the loss of a good many lives — between the hostiles and a party of our troops under Lieutenant George Crook. It finally ended in the establishment of a military post in the vicinity of the battle-ground, for the permanent occupation of the country.

A great load was lifted from my heart when I found myself so near Williamson's camp, which I joined August 4, 1855, receiving a warm welcome from the officers. During the afternoon I relieved Lieutenant Hood of the command of the personal escort, and he was ordered to return, with twelve of the mounted men, over the trail I had followed. I pointed out to him on the map the spot where he would find the two men left on the roadside, and he was directed to take them into Fort Reading. They were found without difficulty, and carried in to the post. The sick man—Duryea—whom I had expected never to see again, afterward became the hospital steward at Fort Yamhill, Oregon, when I was stationed there.

The Indians that I had passed at the ford came to the bluff above the camp, and arranging themselves in a squatting posture, looked down upon Williamson's party with longing eyes, in expectation of a feast. They were a pitiable lot, almost naked, hungry and cadaverous. Indians are always hungry, but these poor creatures were particularly so, as their usual supply of food had grown very scarce from one cause and another. In prosperity they mainly subsisted on fish, or game killed with the bow and arrow. When these sources failed they lived on grasshoppers, and at this season the grasshopper was their principal food. In former years salmon were very abundant in the streams of the Sacramento Valley, and every fall they took great quantities of these fish and dried them for winter use, but alluvial mining had of late years defiled the water of the different streams and driven the fish out. On this account the usual supply of salmon was very limited. They got some trout high up on the rivers, above the sluices and rockers of the miners, but this was a precarious source from which to derive food, as their means of taking the trout were very primitive. They had neither hooks nor lines, but depended entirely on a contrivance made from long, slender branches of willow, which grew on the banks of most of the streams. One of these branches would be cut, and after sharpening the butt-end to a point, split a certain distance, and by a wedge the prongs divided sufficiently to admit a fish between. The Indian fisherman would then slyly put the forked end in the water over his intended victim, and with a quick dart firmly wedge him between the prongs. When secured there, the work of landing him took but a moment. When trout were plentiful this primitive mode of taking them was quite successful, and I have often known hundreds of pounds to be caught in this way, but when they were scarce and suspicious the rude method was not rewarded with good results.

The band looking down on us evidently had not had much fish or game to eat for some time, so when they had made Williamson understand that they were suffering for food he permitted them to come into camp, and furnished them with a supply, which they greedily swallowed as fast as it was placed at their service, regardless of possible indigestion. When they had eaten all they could hold, their enjoyment was made complete by the soldiers, who gave them a quantity of strong plug tobacco. This they smoked incessantly, inhaling all the smoke, so that none of the effect should be lost. When we abandoned this camp the next day, the miserable wretches remained in it and collected the offal about the cooks' fires to feast still more, piecing out the meal, no doubt, with their staple article of food—grasshoppers.

On the morning of August 5 Lieutenant Hood started back to Fort Reading, and Lieutenant Williamson resumed his march for the Columbia River. Our course was up Pit River, by the lower and upper canons, then across to the Klamath Lakes, then east, along their edge to the upper lake. At the middle Klamath Lake, just after crossing Lost River and the Natural Bridge, we met a small party of citizens from Jacksonville, Oregon, looking for hostile Indians who had committed some depredations in their neighborhood. From them we learned that the Rogue River Indians in southern Oregon were on the war-path, and that as the "regular troops up there were of no account, the citizens had taken matters in hand, and intended cleaning up the hostiles." They swaggered about our camp, bragged a good deal, cursed the Indians loudly, and soundly abused the Government for not giving them better protection. It struck me, however, that they had not worked very hard to find the hostiles; indeed, it could plainly be seen that their expedition was a town-meeting sort of affair, and that anxiety to get safe home was uppermost in their thoughts. The enthusiasm with which they started had all oozed out, and that night they marched back to Jacksonville. The next day, at the head of the lake, we came across an Indian village, and I have often wondered since what would have been the course pursued by these valiant warriors from Jacksonville had they gone far enough to get into its vicinity.

When we reached the village the tepees—made of grass—were all standing, the fires burning and pots boiling—the pots filled with camas and tula roots—but not an Indian was to be seen. Williamson directed that nothing in the village should be disturbed; so guards were placed over it to carry out his instructions and we went into camp just a little beyond. We had scarcely established ourselves when a very old Indian rose up from the high grass some distance off, and with peaceable signs approached our camp, evidently for the purpose of learning whether or not our intentions were hostile. Williamson told him we were friendly; that we had passed through his village without molesting it, that we had put a guard there to secure the property his people had abandoned in their fright, and that they might come back in safety. The old man searchingly eyed everything around for some little time, and gaining confidence from the peaceable appearance of the men, who were engaged in putting up the tents and preparing their evening meal, he concluded to accept our professions of friendship, and bring his people in. Going out about half a mile from the village he gave a peculiar yell, at which between three and four hundred Indians arose simultaneously from the ground, and in answer to his signal came out of the tall grass like a swarm of locusts and soon overran our camp in search of food, for like all Indians they were hungry. They too, proved to be Pit Rivers, and were not less repulsive than those of their tribe we had met before. They were aware of the hostilities going on between the Rogue Rivers and the whites but claimed that they had not taken any part in them. I question if they had, but had our party been small, I fear we should have been received at their village in a very different manner.

From the upper Klamath Lake we marched over the divide and down the valley of the Des Chutes River to a point opposite the mountains called the Three Sisters. Here, on September 23, the party divided, Williamson and I crossing through the crater of the Three Sisters and along the western slope of the Cascade Range, until we struck the trail on McKenzie River, which led us into the Willamette Valley not far from Eugene City. We then marched down the Willamette Valley to Portland, Oregon, where we arrived October 9, 1855.

The infantry portion of the command, escorting Lieutenant Henry L. Abbot, followed farther down the Des Chutes River, to a point opposite Mount Hood, from which it came into the Willamette Valley and then marched to Portland. At Portland we all united, and moving across the point between the Willamette and Columbia rivers, encamped opposite Fort Vancouver, on the south bank of the latter stream, on the farm of an old settler named Switzler, who had located there many years before.

CHAPTER IV.

"OLD RED"—SKILLFUL SHOOTING—YAKIMA WAR—A LUDICROUS MISTAKE
"CUT-MOUTH JOHN'S" ENCOUNTER—FATHER PANDOZA'S MISSION
A SNOW-STORM—FAILURE OF THE EXPEDITION.

OUR CAMP ON THE COLUMBIA, NEAR FORT VANCOUVER, was beautifully situated on a grassy sward close to the great river; and as little duty was required of us after so long a journey, amusement of one kind or another, and an interchange of visit with the officers at the post, filled in the time acceptably. We had in camp an old mountaineer guide who had accompanied us on the recent march, and who had received the *sobriquet* of "Old Red," on account of the shocky and tangled mass of red hair and beard, which covered his head and face so completely that only his eyes could be seen. His eccentricities constantly supplied us with a variety of amusements. Among the pastimes he indulged in was one which exhibited his skill with the rifle, and at the same time protected the camp from the intrusions and ravages of a drove of razor-backed hogs which belonged to Mr. Switzler. These hogs were frequent visitors, and very destructive to our grassy sward, rooting it up in front of our tents and all about us, in pursuit of bulbous roots and offal from the camp. Old Red conceived the idea that it would be well to disable the pigs by shooting off the tips of their snouts, and he proceeded to put his conception into execution, and continued it daily whenever the hogs made their appearance. Of course their owner made a row about it; but when Old Red daily settled for his fun by paying liberally with gold-dust from some small bottles of the precious metal in his possession, Switzler readily became contented, and I think even encouraged the exhibitions of skill.

It was at this period (October, 1855) that the Yakima Indian war broke out, and I was detached from duty with the exploring party and required by Major Gabriel J. Rains, then commanding the district, to join an expedition against the Yakimas. They had some times before killed their agent, and in consequence a force under Major Granville O. Haller had been sent out from the Dalles of the Columbia to chastise them; but the expedition had not been successful; in fact, it had been driven back, losing a number of men and two mountain howitzers.

The object of the second expedition was to retrieve this disaster. The force was composed of a small body of regular troops, and a regiment of Oregon mounted volunteers under command of Colonel James W. Nesmith—subsequently for several years United States Senator from Oregon. The whole force was under the command of Major Rains, Fourth Infantry, who, in order that he might rank Nesmith, by some hocus-pocus had been made a brigadier-general, under an appointment from the Governor of Washington Territory.

We started from the Dalles October 30, under conditions that were not conducive to success. The season was late for operations; and worse still, the command was not in accord with the commanding officer, because of general belief in his incompetency, and on account of the fictitious rank he assumed. On the second day out I struck a small body of Indians with my detachment of dragoons, but was unable to do them any particular injury beyond getting possession of a large quantity of their winter food, which their hurried departure compelled them to abandon. This food consisted principally of dried salmon—pulverized and packed in sacks made of grass—dried huckleberries, and dried camas; the latter a bulbous root about the size of a small onion, which, when roasted and ground, is made into bread by the Indians and has a taste somewhat like cooked chestnuts.

Our objective point was Father Pandoza's Mission, in the Yakima Valley, which could be reached by two different routes, and though celerity of movement was essential, our commanding officer "strategically" adopted the longer route, and thus the Indians had ample opportunity to get away with their horses, cattle, women and children, and camp property.

After the encounter which I just now referred to, the command, which had halted to learn the results of my chase, resumed its march to and through the Klikitat canon, and into the lower Yakima Valley, in the direction of the Yakima River. I had charge at the head of the column as it passed through the canon, and on entering the valley beyond, saw in the distance five or six Indian scouts, whom I pressed very closely, until after a run of several miles they escaped across the Yakima River.

The soil in the valley was light and dry, and the movement of animals over it raised great clouds of dust, that rendered it very difficult to distinguish friend from foe; and as I was now separated from the main column a considerable distance, I deemed it prudent to call a halt until we could discover the direction taken by the principal body of the Indians. We soon learned that they had gone up the valley, and looking that way, we discovered a column of alkali dust approaching us, about a mile distant, interposing between my little detachment and the point where I knew General Rains intended to encamp for the night. After hastily consulting with Lieutenant Edward H. Day, of the Third United States Artillery, who was with me, we both concluded that the dust was caused by a body of the enemy which had slipped in between us and our main force. There seemed no alternative left us but to get back to our friends by charging through these Indians; and as their cloud of dust was much larger than ours, this appeared a desperate chance. Preparations to charge were begun, however, but, much to our surprise, before they were completed the approaching party halted for a moment and then

commenced to retreat. This calmed the throbbing of our hearts, and with a wild cheer we started in a hot pursuit, that continued for about two miles, when to our great relief we discovered that we were driving into Rains' camp a squadron of Nesmith's battalion of Oregon volunteers that we had mistaken for Indians, and who in turn believed us to be the enemy. When camp was reached, we all indulged in a hearty laugh over the affair, and at the fright each party had given the other. The explanations which ensued proved that the squadron of volunteers had separated from the column at the same time that I had when we debouched from the canon, and had pursued an intermediate trail through the hills, which brought it into the valley of the Yakima at a point higher up the river than where I had struck it. Next day we resumed our march up the valley, parallel to the Yakima. About 1 o'clock we saw a large body of Indians on the opposite side of the river, and the general commanding made up his mind to cross and attack them. The stream was cold, deep, and swift, still I succeeded in passing my dragoons over safely, but had hardly got them well on the opposite bank when the Indians swooped down upon us. Dismounting my men, we received the savages with a heavy fire, which brought them to a halt with some damage and more or less confusion.

General Rains now became very much excited and alarmed about me, and endeavored to ford the swift river with his infantry and artillery, but soon had to abandon the attempt, as three or four of the poor fellows were swept off their feet and drowned. Meantime Nesmith came up with his mounted force, crossed over, and joined me.

The Indians now fell back to a high ridge, on the crest of which they marched and counter-marched, threatening to charge down its face. Most of them were naked, and as their persons were painted in gaudy colors and decorated with strips of red flannel, red blankets and gay war-bonnets, their appearance presented a scent of picturesque

barbarism, fascinating but repulsive. As they numbered about six hundred, the chances of whipping them did not seem overwhelmingly in our favor, yet Nesmith and I concluded we would give them a little fight, provided we could engage them without going beyond the ridge. But all our efforts were in vain, for as we advanced they retreated, and as we drew back they reappeared and renewed their parade and noisy demonstrations, all the time beating their drums and yelling lustily. They could not be tempted into a fight where we desired it, however, and as we felt unequal to any pursuit beyond the ridge without the assistance of the infantry and artillery, we recrossed the river and encamped with Rains. It soon became apparent that the noisy demonstrations of the Indians were intended only as a blind to cover the escape of their women and children to a place of safety in the mountains.

Next morning we took up our march without crossing the river; and as our route would lead us by the point on the opposite bank where the Indians had made their picturesque display the day before, they at an early hour came over to our side, and rapidly moved ahead of us to some distant hills, leaving in our pathway some of the more venturesome young braves, who attempted to retard our advance by opening fire at long range from favorable places where they lay concealed. This fire did us little harm, but it had the effect of making our progress so slow that the patience of every one but General Rains was well-nigh exhausted.

About 2 o'clock in the afternoon we arrived well up near the base of the range of hills, and though it was growing late we still had time to accomplish something, but our commanding officer decided that it was best to go into camp, and make a systematic attack next morning. I proposed that he let me charge with my dragoons through the narrow canon where the river broke through the range, while the infantry should charge up the hill and drive the enemy from the top down on the other side. In this way I thought we might possibly catch some of

the fugitives, but his extreme caution led him to refuse the suggestion, so we pitched our tents out of range of their desultory fire, but near enough to observe plainly their menacing and tantalizing exhibitions of contempt.

In addition to firing occasionally, they called us all sorts of bad names, made indecent gestures, and aggravated us, so that between 3 and 4 o'clock in the afternoon, by an inexplicable concert of action, and with a serious breach of discipline, a large number of the men and many of the officers broke *en masse* from the camp with loud yells and charged the offending savages. As soon as this mob got within musket-shot they opened fire on the Indians, who ran down the other face of the ridge without making the slightest resistance. The hill was readily taken by this unmilitary proceeding, and no one was hurt on either side, but as Rains would not permit it to be held, a large bonfire was lighted on the crest in celebration of the victory, and then all hands marched back to camp, where they had no sooner arrived and got settled down than the Indians returned to the summit of the ridge, seemingly to enjoy the fire that had been so generously built for their benefit, and with renewed taunts and gestures continued to insult us.

Our camp that night was stongly picketed, and when we awoke in the morning the Indians still occupied their position on the hill. At daylight we advanced against them, two or three companies of infantry moving forward to drive them from the summit, while our main column passed through the canon into the upper Yakima Valley led by my dragoons, who were not allowed to charge into the gorge, as the celerity of such a movement might cause the tactical combination to fail.

As we passed slowly and cautiously through the canon the Indians ran rapidly away, and when we reached the farther end they had entirely disappeared from our front, except one old fellow, whose lame horse prevented him keeping up with the main body. This presented an opportunity for gaining results which all thought should

not be lost, so our guide, an Indian named "Cut-mouth John," seized upon it, and giving hot chase, soon overtook the poor creature, whom he speedily killed without much danger to himself, for the fugitive was armed with only an old Hudson's Bay flint-lock horse-pistol which could not be discharged.

"Cut-mouth John's" engagement began and ended all the fighting that took place on this occasion, and much disappointment and discontent followed, Nesmith's mounted force and my dragoons being particularly disgusted because they had not been "given a chance." During the remainder of the day we cautiously followed the retreating foe, and late in the evening went into camp a short distance from Father Pandoza's Mission, where we were to await a small column of troops under command of Captain Maurice Maloney, of the Fourth Infantry, that was to join us from Steilicoom by way of the Natchez Pass, and from which no tidings had as yet been received.

Next morning the first thing I saw when I put my head out from my blankets was "Cut-mouth John," already mounted and parading himself through the camp. The scalp of the Indian he had despatched the day before was tied to the cross-bar of his bridle bit, the hair dangling almost to the ground, and John was decked out in the sacred vestments of Father Pandoza, having, long before any one was stirring in camp, ransacked the log-cabin at the Mission in which the good man had lived. John was at all times a most repulsive looking individual, a part of his mouth having been shot away in a fight with Indians near Walla Walla some years before, in which a Methodist missionary had been killed; but his revolting personal appearance was now worse than ever, and the sacreligious use of Father Pandoza's vestments, coupled with the ghastly scalp that hung from his bridle, so turned opinion against him that he was soon captured, dismounted, and his parade brought to an abrupt close, and I doubt whether he ever after quite reinstated himself in the good graces of the command.

In the course of the day nearly all the men visited the Mission, but as it had been plundered by the Indians at the outbreak of hostilities, when Father Pandoza was carried off, little of value was left about it except a considerable herd of pigs, which the father with great difficulty had succeeded in accumulating from a very small beginning. The pigs had not been disturbed by the cabbages and potatoes in the garden, with the intention, no doubt, of dining that day on fresh pork and fresh vegetables instead of on salt junk and hard bread, which formed their regular diet on the march. In digging up the potatoes some one discovered half a keg of powder, which had been buried in the garden by the good father to prevent the hostile Indians from getting it to use against the whites. As soon as this was unearthed wild excitement ensued, and a cry arose that Father Pandoza was the person who furnished powder to the Indians; that here was the proof; that at last the mysterious means by which the Indians obtained ammunition was explained—and a rush was made for the mission building. This was a comfortable log-house of good size, built by the Indians for a school and church, and attached to one end was the log-cabin residence of the priest. Its destruction was a matter of but a few moments. A large heap of dry wood was quickly collected and piled in the building, matches applied, and the whole Mission, including the priest's house, was soon enveloped in flames, and burned to the ground before the officers in camp became aware of the disgraceful plundering in which their men were engaged.

The commanding officer having received no news from Captain Maloney during the day, Colonel Nesmith and I were ordered to go to his rescue, as it was concluded that he had been surrounded by Indians in the Natchez Pass. We started early the next morning, the snow falling slightly as we set out, and soon arrived at the eastern mouth of the Natchez Pass. On the way we noticed an abandoned Indian village, which had evidently not been occupied for some time. As we proceeded the storm increased, and the snow-fall became deeper and deeper, until finally our horses could not travel through it. In consequence we were compelled to give up further efforts to advance, and obliged to turn back to the abandoned village, where we encamped for the night. Near night-fall the storm greatly increased, and our bivouac became most uncomfortable; but spreading my blankets on the snow and covering them with Indian matting, I turned in and slept with that soundness and refreshment accorded by nature to one exhausted by fatigue. When I awoke in the morning I found myself under about two feet of snow, from which I arose with difficulty, yet grateful that it had kept me warm during the night.

After a cup of coffee and a little hard bread, it was decided we should return to the main camp near the mission, for we were now confident that Maloney was delayed by the snow, and safe enough on the other side of the mountains. At all events he was beyond aid from us, for the impassable snow-drifts could not be overcome with the means in our possession. It turned out that our suppositions as to the cause of his delay were correct. He had met with the same difficulties that confronted us, and had been compelled to go into camp.

Meanwhile valuable time had been lost, and the Indians, with their families and stock, were well on their way to the Okenagan [*sic*] country, a region into which we could not penetrate in the winter season. No other course was therefore left but to complete the dismal failure of the expedition by returning home, and our commander readily gave the order to march back to the Dalles by the "short" route over the Yakima Mountains.

As the storm was still unabated, it was evident our march home would be a most difficult one, and it was deemed advisable to start back at once, lest we should be blocked up in the mountains by the snows for a period beyond which our provisions would not last. Relying on the fact that the short route to the Dalles would lead us over the range at its most depressed point, where it was hoped the depth of snow was not yet so great as to make the route impassable, we started with Colonel Nesmith's battalion in advance to break the road, followed by my dragoons. In the valley we made rapid progress, but when we reached the mountain every step we took up its side showed the snow to be growing deeper and deeper. At last Nesmith reached the summit, and there found a depth of about six feet of snow covering the plateau in every direction, concealing all signs of the trail so thoroughly that his guides became bewildered and took the wrong divide. The moment I arrived at the top my guide—Donald McKay—who knew perfectly the whole Yakima range, discovered Nesmith's mistake. Word was sent to bring him back, but as he had already nearly crossed the plateau, considerable delay occurred before he returned. When he arrived we began anew the work of breaking a road for the foot troops behind us, my detachment now in advance. The deep snow made our work extremely laborious, exhausting men and horses almost to the point of relinquishing the struggle, but our desperate situation required that we should get down into the valley beyond, or run the chance of perishing on the mountain in a storm which seemed unending. About midnight the column reached the valley, very tired and hungry, but much elated over its escape. We had spent a day of the most intense anxiety, especially those who had had the responsibility of keeping to the right trail, and been charged with the hard work of breaking the road for the infantry and artillery through such a depth of snow.

Our main difficulties were now over, and in due time we reached the Dalles, which almost everyone connected with the expedition voted it a wretched failure, indeed, General Rains himself could not think otherwise, but he scattered far and wide blame for the failure of his combinations. This, of course, led to criminations and recriminations, which eventuated in charges of incompetency preferred gainst him by Captain Edward O.C. Ord, of the Third Artillery. Rains met the charges with counter-charges against Ord, whom he accused of purloining Father Pandoza's shoes, when the soldiers in their fury about the ammunition destroyed the Mission. At the time of its destruction a rumor of this nature was circulated through camp, started by some wag, no doubt in jest; for Ord, who was somewhat eccentric in his habits, and had started on the expedition rather indifferently shod in carpet-slippers, here came out in a brand-new pair of shoes. Of course there was no real foundation for such a report, but Rains was not above small things, as the bringing of this petty accusation attests. Neither party was ever tried, for General John E. Wool, the department commander, had not at command a sufficient number of officers of appropriate rank to constitute a court in the case of Rains, and the charges against Ord were very properly ignored on account of their trifling character.

Shortly after the expedition returned to the Dalles, my detachment was sent down to Fort Vancouver, and I remained at that post during the winter of 1855-56, till late in March.

CHAPTER V.

HE FAILURE OF THE HALLER EXPEDITION FROM LACK OF a sufficient force, and of the Rains expedition from the incompetency of its commander, was a great mortification to the officers and men connected with them, and, taken together, had a marked effect upon the Indian situation in Oregon and Washington Territories at that particular era. Besides, it led to further complications and troubles, for it had begun to dawn upon the Indians that the whites wanted to come in and dispossess them of their lands and homes, and the failures of Haller and Rains fostered the belief with the Indians that they could successfully resist the pressure of civilization.

Acting under these influences, the Spokanes, Walla Wallas, Umatillas, and Nez Perces cast their lot with the hostiles, and all the savage inhabitants of the region east of the Cascade Range became involved in a dispute as to whether the Indians or the Government should possess certain sections of the country, which finally culminated in the war of 1856.

Partly to meet the situation that was approaching, the Ninth Infantry had been sent out from the Atlantic coast to Washington Territory, and upon its arrival at Fort Vancouver encamped in front of the officers' quarters, on the beautiful parade-ground of that post, and set about preparing for the coming campaign. The commander,

Colonel George Wright, who had been promoted to the colonelcy of the regiment upon its organization the previous year, had seen much active duty since his graduation over thirty years before, serving with credit in the Florida and Mexican wars. For the three years previous to his assignment to the Ninth Infantry he had been stationed on the Pacific coast, and the experience he had there acquired, added to his excellent soldierly qualities, was of much benefit in the active campaigns in which, during the following years, he was to participate. Subsequently his career was brought to an untimely close when, nine years after this period, as he was returning to the scene of his successes, he, in common with many others was drowned by the wreck of the ill-fated steamer *Brother Jonathan*. Colonel Wright took command of this district in place of Rains, and had been at Vancouver but a short time before he realized that it would be necessary to fight the confederated tribes east of the Cascade Range of mountains, in order to disabuse them of the idea that they were sufficiently strong to cope with the power of the Government. He therefore at once set about the work of organizing and equipping his troops for a start in the early spring against the hostile Indians, intending to make the objective point of his expedition the heart of the Spokane country on the Upper Columbia River, as the head and front of the confederation was represented in the person of old Cammiackan, chief of the Spokanes.

The regiment moved from Fort Vancouver by boat, March 25, 1856, and landed at the small town called the Dalles, below the mouth of the Des Chutes River at the eastern base of the Cascade Range, and just above where the Columbia River enters those mountains. This rendezvous was to be the immediate point of departure, and all the troops composing the expedition were concentrated there.

On the morning of March 26 the movement began, but the column had only reached Five Mile Creek when the Yakimas, joined by many young warriors—free lances—from other tribes, made a sudden and unexpected attack at the Cascades of the Columbia, midway between Vancouver and the Dalles, killed several citizens, women and children, and took possession of the Portage by besieging the settlers in their cabins at the Upper Cascades, and those who sought shelter at the Middle Cascades in the old military block-house which had been built some years before as a place of refuge under just such circumstances. These points held out, and were not captured, but the landing at the Lower Cascades fell completely into the hands of the savages. Straggling settlers from the Lower Cascades made their way down to Fort Vancouver, distant about thirty-six miles, which they reached that night, and communicated the condition of affairs. As the necessity for early relief to the settlers and the re-establishment of communication with the Dalles were apparent, all the force that could be spared was ordered out, and in condequence I immediately received directions to go with my detachment of dragoons, numbering about forty effective men, to the relief of the middle block-house, which really meant to retake the Cascades. I got ready at once, and believing that a piece of artillery would be of service to me, asked for one, but as there proved to be no guns at the post, I should have been obliged to proceed without one had it not been that the regular steamer from San Francisco to Portland was lying at the Vancouver dock unloading military supplies, and the commander, Captain Dall, supplied me with the steamer's small iron cannon, mounted on a wooden platform, which he used in firing salutes at different ports on the arrival and departure of the vessel. Finding at the arsenal a supply of solid shot that would fit the gun, I had it put upon the steamboat *Belle*, employed to carry my command to the scene of operations, and started up the Columbia River at 2 a.m. on the morning of the 27th. We reached the Lower Cascades early in the day, where, selecting a favorable place for the purpose, I disembarked my men and gun on the north bank of the river, so that I could send back the steamboat to bring up any volunteer assistance that in the mean time might have been collected at Vancouver.

The Columbia River was very high at the time, and the water had backed up into the slough about the foot of the Lower Cascades to such a degree that it left me only a narrow neck of firm ground to advance over toward the point occupied by the Indians. On this neck of land the hostiles had taken position, as I soon learned by frequent shots, loud shouting, and much blustering; they, by the most exasperating yells and indecent exhibitions, daring me to the contest.

After getting well in hand everything connected with my little command, I advanced with five or six men to the edge of a growth of underbrush to make a reconnoissance. We stole along under cover of this underbrush until we reached the open ground leading over the causeway or narrow neck before mentioned, when the enemy opened fire and killed a soldier near my side by a shot which, just grazing the bridge of my nose, struck him in the neck, opening an artery and breaking the spinal cord. He died instantly. The Indians at once made a rush for the body, but my men in the rear, coming quickly to the rescue, drove them back; and Captain Dall's gun being now brought into play, many solid shots were thrown into the jungle where they lay concealed, with the effect of considerably moderating their impetuousity. Further skirmishing at a long range took place at intervals during the day, with little gain or loss, however, to either side, for both parties held positions which could not be assailed in flank, and only the extreme of rashness in either could prompt a front attack. My left was protected by the back water driven into the slough by the high stage of the river, and my right rested secure on the main stream. Between us was only the narrow neck of land, to cross which would be certain death. The position of the Indians was almost the exact counterpart of ours.

In the evening I sent a report of the situation back to Vancouver by the steamboat, retaining a large Hudson's Bay bateau which I had brought up with me. Examining this I found it would carry about twenty men, and made up my mind that early next morning I would cross the command to the opposite or south side of the Columbia River, and make my way up along the mountain base until I arrived abreast the middle block-house, which was still closely beseiged, and then at some favorable point recross to the north bank to its relief, endeavoring in this manner to pass around and to the rear of the Indians, whose position confronting me was too strong for a direct attack. This plan was hazardous, but I believed it could be successfully carried out if the boat could be taken with me; but should I not be able to do this I felt that the object contemplated in sending me out would miserably fail, and the small band cooped up at the block-house would soon starve or fall a prey to the Indians, so I concluded to risk all the chances the plan involved.

On the morning of March 28 the savages were still in my front, and after giving them some solid shot from Captain Dall's gun we slipped down to the river-bank, and the detachment crossed by means of the Hudson's Bay boat, making a landing on the opposite shore at a point where the south channel of the river, after flowing around Bradford's Island, joins the main stream. It was then about 9 o'clock, and everything had thus far proceeded favorably, but an examination of the channel showed that it would be impossible to get the boat up the rapids along the mainland, and that success could only be assured by crossing the south channel just below the rapids to the island, along the shore of which there was every probability we could pull the boat through the rocks and swift water until the head of the rapids was reached, from which point to the block-house there was smooth water.

Telling the men of the embarrassment in which I found myself, and that if I could get enough of them to man the boat and pull it up the stream by a rope to the shore we would cross to the island and make the attempt, all volunteered to go, but as ten men seemed sufficient I selected that number to accompany me. Before starting, however, I deemed it prudent to find out if possible what was engaging the attention of the Indians, who had not yet discovered that we had left their front. I therefore climbed up the side of the abrupt mountain which skirted the water's edge until I could see across the island. From this point I observed the Indians running horse-races and otherwise enjoying themselves behind the line they had held against me the day before. The squaws decked out in gay colors, and the men gaudily dressed in war bonnets, made the scene most attractive, but as everything looked propitious for the dangerous enterprise in hand I spent little time watching them. Quickly returning to the boat, I crossed to the island with my ten men, threw ashore the rope attached to the bow, and commenced the difficult task of pulling her up the rapids. We got along slowly at first, but soon striking a camp of old squaws who had been left on the island for safety, and had not gone over to the mainland to see the races, we utilized them to our advantage. With unmistakable threats and signs we made them not only keep quiet, but also give us much needed assistance in pulling vigorously on the tow-rope of our boat.

I was laboring under a dreadful strain of mental anxiety during all this time, for had the Indians discovered what we were about, they could easily have come over to the island in their canoes, and, by forcing us to take up our arms to repel their attack, doubtless would have obliged the abandonment of the boat, and that essential adjunct to the final success of my plan would have gone down the rapids. Indeed, under such circumstances, it would have been impossible for ten men to hold out against the two or three hundred Indians; but the island forming an excellent screen to our movements, we were not discovered, and when we reached the smooth water at the upper end of the rapids we quickly crossed over and joined the rest of the men, who in the meantime had worked their way along the south bank of the river parallel with us. I felt very grateful to the old squaws for the assistance they rendered. They worked well under compulsion, and manifested no disposition to strike for higher wages. Indeed, I was so much relieved when we had crossed over from the island and joined the rest of the party, that I mentally thanked the squaws one and all. I had much difficulty in keeping the men on the main shore from cheering at our success, but hurriedly taking into the bateau all of them it could carry, I sent the balance along the southern bank, where the railroad is now built, until both detachments arrived at a point opposite the block-house, when, crossing to the north bank, I landed below the block-house some little distance, and returned the boat for the balance of the men, who joined me in a few minutes.

When the Indians attacked the people at the Cascades on the 26th, word was sent to Colonel Wright, who had already got out from the Dalles a few miles on his expedition to the Spokane country. He immediately turned his column back, and soon after I had landed and communicated with the beleaguered block-house the advance of his command arrived under Lieutenant Colonel Edward J. Steptoe. I reported to Steptoe, and related what had occurred during the past thirty-six hours, gave him a description of the festivities that were going on at the lower Cascades, and also communicated the intelligence that the Yakimas had been joined by the Cascade Indians when the place was first attacked. I also told him it was my belief that when he pushed down the main shore the latter tribe without doubt would cross over to the islands we had just left, while the former would take to the mountains. Steptoe coincided with me in this opinion, and informing me that Lieutenant Alexander Piper would join my detachment with a mountain howitzer, directed me to convey the command to the island and gobble up all who came over to it.

Lieutenant Piper and I landed on the island with the first boatload, and after disembarking the howitzer we fired two or three shots to let the Indians know we had artillery with us, then advanced down the island with the whole of my command, which had arrived in the mean time; all of the men were deployed as skirmishers except a small detachment to operate the howitzer. Near the lower end of the island we met, as I had anticipated, the entire body of Cascade Indians—men, women, and children—whose homes were in the vicinity of the Cascades. They were very much frightened and demoralized at the turn events had taken, for the Yakimas at the approach of Steptoe had abandoned them, as predicted, and fled to the mountains. The chief and head-men said they had had nothing to do with the capture of the Cascades, with the murder of men at the upper landing, nor with the massacre of men, women, and children near the block-house, and put all the blame on the Yakimas and their allies. I did not believe this, however, and to test the truth of their statement formed them all in line with their muskets in hand. Going up to the first man on the right I accused him of having engaged in the massacre, but was met by a vigorous denial. Putting my forefinger into the muzzle of his gun, I found unmistakable signs of its having been recently discharged. My finger was black with the stains of burnt powder, and holding it up to the Indian, he had nothing more to say in the face of such positive evidence of his guilt. A further examination proved that all the guns were in the same condition. Their arms were at once taken possession of, and leaving a small force to look after the women and children and the very old men, so that there could be no possibility of escape, I arrested thirteen of the principal miscreants, crossed the river to the lower landing, and placed them in charge of a strong guard.

Late in the evening the steamboat, which I had sent back to Vancouver, returned, bringing to my assistance from Vancouver, Captain Henry D. Wallen's company of the Fourth Infantry, and a company of volunteers hastily organized at Portland, but as the Cascades had already been retaken, this reinforcement was too late to participate in the affair. The volunteers from Portland, however, were spoiling for a fight, and in the absence of other opportunity desired to shoot the prisoners I held (who, they alleged, had killed a man named Seymour), and proceeded to make their arrangements to do so, only desisting on being informed that the Indians were my prisoners, subject to the orders of Colonel Wright, and would be protected to the last by my detachment. Not long afterward Seymour turned up safe and sound, having fled at the beginning of the attack on the Cascades, and hid somewhere in the thick underbrush until the trouble was over, and then made his way back to the settlement. The next day I turned my prisoners over to Colonel Wright, who had them marched to the upper landing of the Cascades, where, after a trial by a military commission, nine of them were sentenced to death and duly hanged. I did not see them executed, but was afterward informed that in the absence of the usual mechanical apparatus used on such occasions, a tree with a convenient limb, under which two empty barrels were placed, one on top of the other, furnished a rude but certain substitute. In executing the sentence each Indian in turn was made to stand on the top barrel, and after the noose was adjusted the lower barrel was knocked away, and the necessary drop thus obtained. In this way the whole nine were punished. Just before death they all acknowledged their guilt by confessing their participation in the massacre at the block-house, and met their doom with the usual stoicism of their race.

CHAPTER VI.

HILE STILL ENCAMPED AT THE LOWER LANDING, SOME three or four days after the events last recounted, Mr. Joseph Meek, an old frontiersman and guide for emigrant trains through the mountains, came down from the Dalles, on his way to Vancouver, and stopped at my camp to inquire if an Indian named Spencer and his family had passed down to Vancouver since my arrival at the Cascades. Spencer, the head of the family, was a very influential, peaceable Chinook chief, whom Colonel Wright had taken with him from Fort Vancouver as an interpreter and mediator with the Spokanes and other hostile tribes, against which his campaign was directed. He was a good, reliable Indian, and on leaving Vancouver to join Colonel Wright, took his family along, to remain with relatives and friends at Fort Dalles until the return of the expedition. When Wright was compelled to retrace his steps on account of the capture of the Cascades, this family for some reason known only to Spencer, was started by him down the river to their home at Vancouver.

Meek, on seeing the family leave the Dalles, had some misgivings as to their safe arrival at their destination, because of the excited condition of the people about the Cascades; but Spencer seemed to think that his own peaceable and friendly reputation, which was widespread, would protect them; so he parted from his wife and children with little apprehension as to their safety. In reply to Meek's question, I stated that I had not seen Spencer's family, when he remarked, "Well, I fear that they are gone up," a phrase used in that country in early days to mean that they had been killed. I questioned him closely, to elicit further information, but no more could be obtained; for Meek, either through ignorance or the usual taciturnity of his class, did not explain more fully, and when the steamer that had brought the reinforcement started down the river, he took passage for Vancouver, to learn definitely if the Indian family had reached that point. I at once sent to the upper landing, distant about six miles, to make inquiry in regard to the matter, and in a little time my messenger returned with the information that the family had reached that place the day before, and finding that we had driven the hostiles off, continued their journey on foot toward my camp, from which point they expected to go by steamer down the river to Vancouver.

Their non-arrival aroused in me suspicions of foul play, so with all the men I could spare, and accompanied by Lieutenant William T. Welcker, of the Ordnance Corps—a warm and intimate friend—I went in search of the family, deploying the men as skirmishers across the valley, and marching them through the heavy forest where the ground was covered with fallen timber and dense underbrush, in order that no point might escape our attention. The search was continued between the base of the mountain and the river without finding any sign of Spencer's family, until about 3 o'clock in the afternoon, when we discovered them between the upper and lower landing, in a small open space about a mile from the road, all dead—strangled to death with bits of rope. The party consisted of the mother, two youths, three girls, and a baby. They had all been killed by white men, who had probably met the innocent creatures somewhere near the block-house, driven them from the road into the timber, where the cruel murders were committed without provocation, and for no other purpose than the gratification of the inordinate hatred of the Indian that has often existed on the frontier, and which on more than one occasion has failed to distinguish friend from foe. The bodies lay in a semi-circle, and the bits of rope with which the poor wretches had been strangled to death were still around their necks. Each piece of rope—the unwound strand of a heavier piece—was about two feet long, and encircled the neck of its victim with a single knot, that must have been drawn tight by the murderers pulling at the ends. As there had not been quite enough rope to answer for all, the babe was strangled by means of a red silk handkerchief, taken, doubtless, from the neck of its mother. It was a distressing sight. A most cruel outrage had been committed upon unarmed people—our friends and allies—in a spirit of aimless revenge. The perpetrators were citizens living near the middle block-house, whose wives and children had been killed a few days before by the hostiles, but who well knew that these unoffending creatures had had nothing to do with those murders.

In my experience I have been obliged to look upon many cruel scenes in connection with Indian warfare on the Plains since that day, but the effect of this dastardly and revolting crime has never been effaced from my memory. Greater and more atrocious massacres have been committed often by Indians; their savage nature modifies one's ideas, however, as to the inhumanity of their acts, but when such wholesale murder as this is done by whites, and the victims not only innocent, but helpless, no defense can be made for those who perpetrated the crime, if they claim to be civilized beings. It is true the people at the Cascades had suffered much, and that their wives and children had been murdered before their eyes, but to wreak vengeance on Spencer's unoffending family, who had walked into their settlement under the protection of a friendly alliance, was an unparalleled outrage which nothing can justify or extenuate. With as little delay as possible after the horrible discovery, I returned to camp, had boxes made, and next day buried the bodies of these hapless victims of misdirected vengeance.

PHILIP H. SHERIDAN

The summary punishment inflicted on the nine Indians, in their trial and execution, had a most salutary effect on the confederation, and was the entering wedge to its disintegration; and though Colonel Wright's campaign continued during the summer and into the early winter, the subjugation of the allied bands became a comparatively easy matter after the lesson taught the renegades who were captured at the Cascades. My detachment did not accompany Colonel Wright, but remained for some time at the Cascades, and while still there General Wool came up from San Francisco to take a look into the condition of things. From his conversation with me in reference to the affair at the Cascades, I gathered that he was greatly pleased at the service I had performed, and I afterward found that his report of my conduct had so favorably impressed General Scott that that distinguished officer complimented me from the headquarters of the army in general orders.

HEADQUARTERS OF THE ARMY,
 NEW YORK, NOV. 13, 1857.

GENERAL ORDERS, No. 14.

1. In announcing to the army the more recent combats with hostile Indians, in which the gallant conduct of the troops, under, in most cases cirsumstances of great hardship and privation, is entitled to high approbation, the General-in-Chief takes occasion to notice all those of a similar character not mentioned in his General order No. 4, of the current series, which have occurred since the beginning of last year, and to which, since the publication of that order, his attention has been directed. They are too interesting to be omitted. In the order of time, the cases are as follows: * * * * VIII. March 28, 1856, Brevt. Lieut,-Col. Edward J. Steptoe, Ninth Infantry, commanding Companies "A," "E," "F," and "I," same regiment, and detachments of Company "E," First Dragoons, and Company "L," Third Artillery, —in all two hundred men —at the Cascades, W.T., repulsed the Indians in their attack at that place. The troops landed under fire, routing and dispersing the enemy at every point, capturing a large number of their mules and

destroying all their property. Second Lieutenant Philip H. Sheridan, Fourth Infantry, is specially mentioned for his gallantry * * * *.

By command of Brevet Lieutenant-General SCOTT.

[Signed] IRVIN McDOWELL,
Assistant Adjutant-General.

General Wool, while personally supervising matters on the Columbia River, directed a redistribution to some extent of the troops in the district, and shortly before his return to San Francisco I was ordered with my detachment of dragoons to take station on the Grande Ronde Indian Reservation in Yamhill County, Oregon, about twenty-five miles southwest of Dayton, and to relieve from duty at that point Lieutenant William B. Hazen—late brigadier-general and chief signal officer—who had established a camp there some time before. I started for my new station on April 21, and marching by way of Portland and Oregon City, arrived at Hazen's camp April 25. The camp was located in the Coast range of mountains, on the northeast part of the reservation, to which last had been added a section of country that was afterward known as the Siletz reservation. The whole body of land set aside went under the general name of the "Coast reservation," from its skirting the Pacific Ocean for some distance north of Yaquina Bay, and the intention was to establish within its bounds permanent homes for such Indians as might be removed to it. In furtherance of this idea, and to relieve northern California and southwestern Oregon from the roaming, restless bands that kept the people of those sections in a state of constant turmoil, many of the different tribes, still under control but liable to take part in warfare, were removed to the reservation, so that they might be away from the theatre of hostilities.

When I arrived I found that the Rogue River Indians had just been placed upon the reservation, and subsequently the Coquille, Klamath, Modocs, and remnants of the Chinooks were collected there also, the home of the latter being in the Willamette Valley. The number all told amounted to some thousands, scattered over the entire Coast reservation, but about fifteen hundred were located at the Grande Ronde under a charge of an agent, Mr. John F. Miller, a sensible, practical man, who left the entire police control to the military, and attended faithfully to the duty of settling the Indians in the work of cultivating the soil.

As the place was to be occupied permanently, Lieutenant Hazen had begun, before my arrival, the erection of buildings for the shelter of his command, and I continued the work of constructing the post as laid out by him. In those days the Government did not provide very liberally for sheltering its soldiers; and officers and men were frequently forced to eke out parsimonious appropriations by toilsome work or go without shelter in most inhospitable regions. Of course this post was no exception to the general rule, and as all hands were occupied in its construction, and I the only officer present, I was kept busily employed in supervising matters, both as commandant and quartermaster, until July, when Captain D. A. Russell, of the Fourth Infantry, was ordered to take command, and I was relieved from the first part of my duties.

About this time my little detachment parted from me, being ordered to join a company of the First Dragoons, commanded by Captain Robert Williams, as it passed up the country from California by way of Yamhill. I regretted exceedingly to see them go, for their faithful work and gallant service had endeared every man to me by the strongest ties. Since I relieved Lieutenant Hood on Pit River, nearly a twelvemonth before, they had been my constant companions, and the zeal with which they had responded to every call I made on them had inspired in my heart a deep affection that years have not removed. When I relieved Hood—a dragoon officer of their own regiment—they did not like the change, and I understood that they somewhat contemptuously expressed this in more ways than one, in order to try the temper of the new "Leftenant," but appreciative and unremitting care, together with firm and just discipline, soon quieted all symptoms of dissatisfaction and overcame all prejudice. The detachment had been made up of details from the different companies of the regiment in order to give Williamson a mounted force, and as it was usual, under such circumstances, for every company commander to shove into the detail he was called upon to furnish the most troublesome and insubordinate individuals of his company, I had some difficulty, when first taking command, in controlling such a medley of recalcitrants; but by forethought for them and their wants, and a strict watchfulness for their rights and comfort, I was able in a short time to make them obedient and the detachment cohesive. In the past year they had made long and tiresome marches, forded swift mountain streams, constructed rafts of logs or bundles of dry reeds to ferry our baggage, swum deep rivers, marched on foot to save their worn-out and exhausted animals, climbed mountains, fought Indians, and in all and everything had done the best they could for the service and their commander. The disaffected feeling they entertained when I first assumed command soon wore away, and in its place came a confidence and respect which it gives me the greatest pleasure to remember, for small though it was, this was my first cavalry command. They little thought, when we were in the mountains of California and Oregon—nor did I myself then dream—that but a few years were to elapse before it would be my lot again to command dragoons, this time in numbers so vast as of themselves to compose almost an army.

Shortly after the arrival of Captain Russell a portion of the Indians at the Grande Ronde reservation were taken down the coast to the Siletz reservation, and I was transferred temporarily to Fort Haskins, on the latter reserve, and assigned to the duty of completing it and building a block-house for the police control of the Indians placed there.

While directing this work, I undertook to make a road across the coast mountains from King's Valley to the Siletz, to shorten the haul between the two points by a route I had explored. I knew there were many obstacles in the way, but the gain would be great if we could overcome them, so I set to work with the enthusiasm of a young pathfinder. The point at which the road was to cross the range was rough and precipitous, but the principal difficulty in making it would be from heavy timber on the mountains that had been burned over years and years before, until nothing was left but limbless trunks of dead trees—firs and pines-that had fallen from time to time until the ground was matted with huge logs from five to eight feet in diameter. These could not be chopped with axes nor sawed by any ordinary means, therefore we had to burn them into suitable lengths, and drag the sections to either side of the roadway with from four to six yoke of oxen.

The work was both tedious and laborious, but in time perseverance surmounted all obstacles and the road was finished, though its grades were very steep. As soon as it was completed, I wished to demonstrate its value practically, so I started a Government wagon over it loaded with about fifteen hundred pounds of freight drawn by six yoke of oxen, and escorted by a small detachment of soldiers. When it had gone about seven miles the sergeant in charge came back to the post and reported his inability to get any further. Going out to the scene of difficulty I found the wagon at the base of a steep hill, stalled. Taking up a whip myself, I directed the men to lay on their gads, for each man had supplied himself with a flexible hickory withe in the early stages of the trip, to start the team, but this course did not move the wagon nor have much effect on the demoralized oxen; but following as a last resort an example I heard of on a former occasion, that brought into use the rough language of the country, I induced the oxen to move with alacrity, and the wagon and contents were speedily carried to the summit. The whole trouble was at once revealed: the oxen had been broken and trained by a man who, when they were in a pinch, had encouraged them by his frontier vocabulary, and they could not realize what was expected of them under extraordinary conditions until they heard familiar and possibly profanely urgent phrases. I took the wagon to its destination, but as it was not brought back, even in all the time I was stationed in that country, I think comment on the success of my road is unnecessary.

I spent many happy months at Fort Haskins, remaining there until the post was nearly completed and its garrison increased by the arrival of Captain F.T. Dent—a brother-in-law of Captain Ulysses S. Grant—with his company of the Fourth Infantry, in April, 1857. In the summer of 1856, and while I was still on duty there, the Coquille Indians on the Siletz, and down near the Yaquina Bay, became, on account of hunger and prospective starvation, very much excited and exasperated, getting beyond the control of their agent, and even threatening his life, so a detachment of troops was sent out to set things to rights, and I took command of it. I took with me most of the company, and arrived at Yaquina Bay in time to succor the agent, who for some days had been besieged in a log hut by the Indians and had almost abandoned hope of rescue.

Having brought with me over the mounatins a few head of beef cattle for the hungry Indians, without thinking of running any great personal risk I had six beeves killed some little distance from my camp, guarding the meat with four soldiers, whom I was obliged to post as sentinels around the small area on which the carcasses lay. The Indians soon formed a circle about the sentinels, and impelled by starvation, attempted to take the beef before it could be equally divided. This was of course resisted, when they drew their knives—their guns having been previously taken away from them—and some of the inferior chiefs gave the signal to attack. The principal chief, Tetooney John, and two other Indians joined me in the centre of the circle, and protesting that they would die rather than that the frenzied onslaught should succeed, harangued the Indians until the rest of the company hastened up from camp and put an end to the disturbance. I always felt grateful to Tetootney John for his loyalty on this occasion, and many times afterward aided his family with a little coffee and sugar, but necessarily surreptitiously, so as not to heighten the prejudices that his friendly act had aroused among his Indian comrades.

The situation at Yaquina Bay did not seem very safe, notwithstanding the supply of beef we brought; and the possibility that the starving Indians might break out was ever present, so to anticipate any further revolt, I called for more troops. The request was complied with by sending to my assistance the greater part of my own company ("K") from Fort Yamhill. The men, inspired by the urgency of our situation, marched more than forty miles a day, accomplishing the whole distance in so short a period, that I doubt if the record has ever been beaten. When this reinforcement arrived, the Indians saw the futility of further demonstrations against their agent, who they seemed to think was responsible for the insufficiency of food, and managed to exist with the slender rations we could spare and such indifferent food as they could pick up, until the Indian Department succeeded in getting up its regular supplies. In the past the poor things had often been pinched by hunger and neglect, and at times their only food was rock oysters, clams and crabs. Great quantities of these shell-fish could be gathered in the bay near at hand, but the mountain Indians, who had heretofore lived on the flesh of mammal, did not take kindly to mollusks, and, indeed, ate the shell-fish only as a last resort.

Crab catching at night on the Yaquina Bay by the coast Indians was a very picturesque scene. It was mostly done by the squaws and children, each equipped with a torch in one hand, and a sharp-pointed stick in the other to take and lift the fish into baskets slung on the back to receive them. I have seen at times hundreds of squaws and children wading about in Yaquina Bay taking crabs in this manner, and the reflection by the water of the light from the many torches, with the movements of the Indians while at work, formed a weird and diverting picture of which we were never tired.

Not long after the arrival of the additional troops from Yamhill, it became apparent that the number of men at Yaquina Bay would have to be reduced, so in view of this necessity, it was deemed advisable to build a block-house for the better protection of the agent, and I looked about for suitable ground on which to erect it. Nearly all around the bay the land rose up from the beach very abruptly, and the only good site that could be found was some level ground used as the burial-place of the Yaquina Bay Indians—a small band of fish-eating people who had lived near this point on the coast for ages. They were a robust lot, of tall and well-shaped figures, and were called in the Chinook tongue "salt chuck," which means fish-eaters, or eaters of food from the salt water. Many of the young men and women were handsome in feature below the forehead, having fine eyes, aquiline noses and good mouths, but, in conformity with a long-standing custom, all had flat heads, which gave them a distorted and hideous appearance, particularly some of the women, who went to the extreme of fashion and flattened the head to the rear in a sharp horizontal ridge by confining it between two boards, one running back from the forehead at an angle of about forty degrees, and the other up perpendicularly from the back of the neck. When a head had been shaped artistically the dusky maiden owner was marked as a belle, and one could become reconciled to it after a time, but when carelessness and neglect had governed in the adjustment of the boards, there probably was nothing in the form of a human being on the face of the earth that appeared so ugly.

It was the mortuary ground of these Indians that occupied the only level spot we could get for the block-house. Their dead were buried in canoes, which rested in the crotches of forked sticks a few feet above-ground. The graveyard was not large, containing probably from forty to fifty canoes in a fair state of preservation. According to the custom of all Indian tribes on the Pacific coast, when one of their number died all his worldly effects were buried with him, so that the canoes were filled with old clothes, blankets, pieces of calico and the like, intended for the use of the departed in the happy hunting-grounds.

I made known to the Indians that we would have to take this piece of ground for the block-house. They demurred at first, for there is nothing more painful to an Indian than disturbing his dead, but they finally consented to hold a council next day on the beach, and thus come to some definite conclusion. Next morning they all assembled, and we talked in the Chinook language all day long, until at last they gave in, consenting, probably, as much because they could not help themselves, as for any other reason. It was agreed that on the following day at 12 o'clock, when the tide was going out, I should take my men and place the canoes in the bay, and let them float out on the tide across the ocean to the happy hunting-grounds.

At that day there existed in Oregon in vast numbers a species of wood-rat, and our inspection of the graveyard showed that the canoes were thickly infested with them. They were a light gray animal, larger than the common gray squirrel, with beautiful bushy tails, which made them strikingly resemble the squirrel, but in cunning and deviltry they were much ahead of that quick-witted rodent. I have known them to empty in one night a keg of spikes in the storehouse in Yamhill, distributing them along the stringers of the building, with apparently no other purpose than amusement. We anticipated great fun watching the efforts of these rats to escape the next day when the canoes should be launched on the ocean, and I therefore forbade any of the command to visit the graveyard in the interim, lest the rats should be alarmed. I well knew that they would not be disturbed by the Indians, who held the sacred spot in awe. When the work of tak-ing down the canoes and carrying them to the water began, expectation was on tiptoe, but, strange as it may seem, not a rat was to be seen. This unexpected developoment was mystifying. They had all disappeared; there was not one in any of the canoes, as investigation proved, for disappointment instigated a most thorough search. The Indians said the rats understood Chinook, and that as they had no wish to accompany the dead across the ocean to the happy hunting-grounds, they took to the woods for safety. However that may be, I have no doubt that the preceding visits to the burial-ground, and our long talk of the day before, with the unusual stir and bustle, had so alarmed the rats that, impelled by their suspicious instincts, they fled a danger, the nature of which they could not anticipate, but which they felt to be none the less real and impending.

CHAPTER VII.

HE TROUBLES AT THE SILETZ AND YAQUINA BAY WERE settled without further excitement by the arrival in due time of plenty of food, and as the buildings at Fort Haskins were so near completion that my services as quartermaster were no longer needed, I was ordered to join my own company at Fort Yamhill, where Captain Russell was still in command. I returned to that place in May, 1857, and at a period a little later, in consequence of the close of hostilities in southern Oregon, the Klamaths and Modocs were sent back to their own country, to that section in which occurred, in 1873, the disastrous war with the latter tribe. This reduced considerably the number of Indians at the Grande Ronde, but as those remaining were still somewhat unruly, from the fact that many questions requiring adjustment were constantly arising between the different bands, the agent and the officers at the post were kept pretty well occupied. Captain Russell assigned to me the special work of keeping up the police control, and as I had learned at an early day to speak Chinook (the "court language" among the coast tribes) almost as well as the Indians themselves, I was thereby enabled to steer my way successfully on many critical occasions.

For some time the most disturbing and most troublesome element we had was the Rogue River band. For three or four years they had fought our troops obstinately, and surrendered at the bitter end in the belief that they were merely over-powered, not conquered. They openly boasted to the other Indians that they could whip the soldiers, and that they did not wish to follow the white man's ways, continuing consistently their wild habits, unmindful of all admonitions. Indeed, they often destroyed their household utensils, tepees and clothing, and killed their horses on the graves of the dead, in the fulfillment of a superstitious custom, which demanded that they should undergo, while mourning for their kindred, the deepest privation in a property sense. Everything the loss of which would make them poor was sacrificed on the graves of their relatives of distinguished warriors, and as melancholy because of removal from their old homes caused frequent deaths, there was no lack of occasion for the sacrifices. The widows and orphans of the dead warriors were of course the chief mourners, and exhibited their grief in many peculiar ways. I remember one in particular which was universally practiced by the near kinsfolk. They would crop their hair very close, and then cover the head with a sort of hood or plaster of black pitch, the composition being clay, pulverized charcoal, and the resinous gum which exudes from the pine-tree. The hood, nearly an inch in thickness, was worn during a period of mourning that lasted through the time it would take nature, by the growth of the hair, actually to lift from the head the heavy covering of pitch after it had become solidified and hard as stone. It must be admitted that they underwent considerable discomfort in memory of their relatives. It took all the influence we could bring to bear to break up these absurdly superstitious practices, and it looked as if no permanent improvement could be effected, for as soon as we got them to discard one, another would be invented. When not allowed to burn down their tepees or houses, those poor souls who were in a dying condition would be carried out to the neighboring hillsides just before dissolution, and there abandoned to their sufferings, with little or no attention, unless the placing under their heads of a small stick of wood—with possibly some laudable object, but doubtless great discomfort to their victim — might be considered such.

To uproot these senseless and monstrous practices was indeed most difficult. The most pernicious of all was one which was likely to bring about tragic results. They believed firmly in a class of doctors among their people who professed that they could procure the illness of an individual at will, and that by certain incantations they could kill or cure the sick person. Their faith in this superstition was so steadfast that there was no doubting its sincerity, many indulging at times in the most trying privations, that their relatives might be saved from death at the hands of the doctors. I often talked with them on the subject, and tried to reason them out of the superstitious belief, defying the doctors to kill me, or even make me ill; but my talks were unavailing, and they always met my arguments with the remark that I was a white man, of a race wholly different from the red man, and that that was the reason the medicine of the doctors would not affect me. These villainous doctors might be either men or women, and any one of them finding an Indian ill, at once averred that his influence was the cause, offering at the same time to cure the invalid for a fee, which generally amounted to about all the ponies his family possessed. If the proposition was accepted and the fee paid over, the family, in case the man died, was to have indemnity through the death of the doctor, who freely promised that they might take his life in such event, relying on his chances of getting protection from the furious relatives by fleeing to the military post till time had so assuaged their grief that matters could be compromised or settled by a restoration of a part of the property, when the rascally leeches could again resume their practice. Of course the services of a doctor were always accepted when an Indian fell ill; otherwise the invalid's death would surely ensue, brought about by the evil influence that was unpropitiated. Latterly it had become quite the thing, when a patient died, for the doctor to flee to our camp — it was so convenient and so much safer than elsewhere—and my cellar was a favorite place of refuge from the infuriated friends of the deceased.

Among the most notable of these doctors was an Indian named Sam Patch, who several times sought asylum in my cellar, and being a most profound diplomat, managed on each occasion and with little delay to negotiate a peaceful settlement and go forth in safety to resume the practice of his nefarious profession. I often hoped he would be caught before reaching the post, but he seemed to know intuitively when the time had come to take leg-bail, for his advent at the garrison generally preceded by but a few hours the death of some poor dupe.

Finally these peculiar customs brought about the punishment of a noted doctress of the Rogue River tribe, a woman who was constantly working in this professional way, and who had found a victim of such prominence among the Rogue Rivers that his unlooked for death brought down on her the wrath of all. She had made him so ill, they believed, as to bring him to death's door notwithstanding the many ponies that had been given her to cease the incantations, and it was the conviction of all that she had finally caused the man's death from some ulterior and indescernible motive. His relatives and friends then immediately set about requiting her with the just penalties of a perfidious breach of contract. Their threats induced her instant flight toward my house for the usual protection, but the enraged friends of the dead man gave hot chase, and overtook the witch just inside the limits of the garrison, where, on the parade-ground, in sight of the officers' quarters, and before any one could interfere, they killed her. There were sixteen men in pursuit of the doctress, and sixteen gunshot wounds were found in her body when examined by the surgeon of the post. The killing of the woman was a flagrant and defiant outrage committed in the teeth of the military authority, yet done so quickly that we could not prevent it. This necessitated severe measures, both to allay the prevailing excitement and to preclude the recurrence of such acts. The body was cared for, and delivered to the relatives the next day for burial, after which Captain Russell directed me to take such steps as would put a stop to the fanatical usages that had brought about this murderous occurrence, for it was now seen that if timely measures were not taken to repress them, similar tragedies would surely follow.

Knowing all the men of the Rogue River tribe, and speaking fluently the Chinook tongue, which they all understood, I went down to their village the following day, after having sent word to the tribe that I wished to have a council with them. The Indians all met me in council, as I had desired, and I then told them that the men who had taken part in shooting the woman would have to be delivered up for punishment. They were very stiff with me at the interview, and with all that talent for circumlocution and diplomacy with which the Indian is gifted, endeavored to evade my demands and delay any conclusion. But I was very positive, would hear of no compromise whatever, and demanded that my terms be at once complied with. No one was with me but a sergeant of my company, named Miller, who held my horse, and as the chances of an agreement began to grow remote, I became anxious for our safety. The conversation waxing hot and the Indians gathering close in around me, I unbuttoned the flap of my pistol holster, to be ready for any emergency. When the altercation became most bitter I put my hand to my hip to draw my pistol, but discovered it was gone — stolen by one of the rascals surrounding me. Finding myself unarmed, I modified my tone and manner to correspond with my helpless condition, thus myself assuming the diplomatic side in the parley, in order to gain time. As soon as an opportunity offered, and I could, without too much loss of self-respect, and without damaging my reputation among the Indians, I moved to where the sergeant held my horse, mounted, and crossing the Yamhill River close by, called back in Chinook from the farther bank that the "sixteen men who killed the woman must be delivered up, and my six-shooter also." This was responded to by contemptuous laughter, so I went back to the military post somewhat crestfallen, and made my report of the turn affairs had taken, inwardly longing for another chance to bring the rascally Rogue Rivers to terms.

When I had explained the situation to Captain Russell, he thought that we could not, under any circumstances, overlook this defiant conduct of the Indians, since, unless summarily punished, it would lead to even more serious trouble in the future. I heartily seconded this proposition, and gladly embracing the opportunity it offered, suggested that if he would give me another chance, and let me have the effective force of the garrison, consisting of about fifty men, I would chastise the Rogue Rivers without fail, and that the next day was all the time I required to complete arrangements. He gave me the necessary authority, and I at once set to work to bring about a better state of discipline on the reservation, and to put an end to the practices of the medicine men (having also in view the recovery of my six-shooter and self-respect), by marching to the village and taking the rebellious Indians by force.

In the tribe there was an excellent woman called Tighee Mary (Tighee in Chinook means chief), who by right of inheritance was a kind of queen of the Rogue Rivers. Fearing that the insubordinate conduct of the Indians would precipitate further trouble, she came early the following morning to see me and tell me of the situation. Mary informed me that she had done all in her power to bring the Indians to reason, but without avail, and that they were determined to fight rather than deliver up the sixteen men who had engaged in the shooting. She also apprised me of the fact that they had taken up a position on the Yamhill River, on the direct road between the post and village, where, painted and armed for war, they were awaiting attack.

On this information I concluded it would be best to march to the village by a circuitous route instead of directly, as at first intended, so

I had the ferry-boat belonging to the post floated about a mile and a half down the Yamhill River and there anchored. At 11 o'clock that night I marched my fifty men out of the garrison, in a direction opposite to that of the point held by the Indians, and soon reached the river at the ferryboat. Here I ferried the party over with little delay, and marched them along the side of the mountain, through the underbrush and fallen timber, until, just before daylight, I found that we were immediately in rear of the village, and hence in rear, also, of the line occupied by the refractory Indians, who were expecting to meet me on the direct road from the post. Just at break of day we made a sudden descent upon the village and took its occupants completely by surprise, even capturing the chief of the tribe, "Sam," who was dressed in all his war toggery, fully armed and equipped, in anticipation of a fight on the road where his comrades were in position. I at once put Sam under guard, giving orders to kill him instantly if the Indians fired a shot; then forming my line on the road beyond the edge of the village, in rear of the force lying in wait for a front attack, we moved forward. When the hostile party realized that they were completely cut off from the village, they came out from their stronghold on the river and took up a line in my front, distant about sixty yards with the apparent intention of resisting to the last.

As is usual with Indians when expecting a fight, they were nearly naked, fantastically painted with blue clay, and hideously arrayed in war bonnets. They seemed very belligerent, brandishing their muskets in the air, dancing on one foot, calling us ugly names, and making such other demonstrations of hostility, that it seemed at first that nothing short of the total destruction of the party could bring about the definite settlement that we were bent on. Still, as it was my desire to bring them under subjection without loss of life, if possible, I determined to see what result would follow when they learned that their chief was at our mercy. So, sending Sam under guard to the front, where he could be seen, informing them that he would be immediately shot if they fired upon us, and aided by the cries and lamentations of the women of the village, who deprecated any hostile action by either party, I soon procured a parley.

The insubordinate Indians were under command of "Joe," Sam's brother, who at last sent me word that he wanted to see me, and we met between our respective lines. I talked kindly to him, but was firm in my demand that the men who killed the woman must be given up and my six-shooter returned. His reply was he did not think it could be done, but he would consult his people. After the consultation, he returned and notified me that fifteen would surrender and the six-shooter would be restored, and further, that we could kill the sixteenth man, since the tribe wished to get rid of him anyhow, adding that he was a bad Indian, whose bullet no doubt had given the woman her death wound. He said that if I assented to this arrangement, he would require all of his people except the objectionable man to run to the right of his line at a preconcerted signal. The bad Indian would be ordered to stand fast on the extreme left, and we could open fire on him as his comrades fell away to the right. I agreed to the proposition, and gave Joe fifteen minutes to execute his part of it. We then returned to our respective forces, and a few minutes later the fifteen ran to the right flank as agreed upon, and we opened fire on the one Indian left standing alone, bringing him down in his tracks severely wounded by a shot through his shoulder.

While all this was going on, the other bands of the reservation, several thousand strong, had occupied the surrounding hills for the purpose of witnessing the fight, for as the Rogue Rivers had been bragging for some time that they could whip the soldiers, these other Indians had come out to see it done. The result, however, disappointed the spectators, and the Rogue Rivers naturally lost caste. The fifteen men now came in and laid down their arms (including my six-shooter) in front of us as agreed, but I compelled them to take the surrendered guns up again and carry them to the post, where they were deposited in the block-house for future security. The prisoners were ironed with ball and chain, and made to work at the post until their rebellious spirit was broken; and the wounded man was correspondingly punished after he had fully recovered. An investigation as to why this man had been selected as the offering by which Joe and his companions expected to gain immunity, showed that the fellow was really a most worthless character, whose death even would have been a benefit to the tribe. Thus it seemed that they had two purposes in view—the one to propititate me and get good terms, the other to rid themselves of a vagabond member of the tribe.

The punishment of these sixteen Indians by ball and chain ended all trouble with the Rogue River tribe. The disturbances arising from the incantations of the doctors and doctresses, and the practice of killing horses and burning all worldly property on the graves of those who died, were completely suppressed, and we made with little effort a great stride toward the civilization of these crude and superstitious people, for they now began to recognize the power of the Government. In their management afterward a course of justice and mild force was adopted, and unvaryingly applied. They were compelled to cultivate their land, to attend church, and to send their children to school. When I saw them, fifteen years later, transformed into industrious and substantial farmers, with neat houses, fine cattle, wagons and horses, carrying their grain, eggs, and butter to market and bringing home flour, coffee, sugar, and calico in return, I found abundant confirmation of my early opinion that the most effectual measures for lifting them from a state of barbarism would be a practical supervision at the outset, coupled with a firm control and mild discipline.

In all that was done for these Indian Captain Russell's judgment and sound, practical ideas were the inspiration. His true manliness, honest and just methods, together with the warm-hearted interest he took in all that pertained to matters of duty to his Government, could not have produced other than the best results, in what position soever he might have been placed. As all the lovable traits of his character were constantly manifested, I became most deeply attached to him, and until the day of his death in 1864, on the battle-field of Opequan, in front of Winchester, while gallantly leading his division under my command, my esteem and affection were sustained and intensified by the same strong bonds that drew me to him in these early days in Oregon.

After the events just narrated I continued on duty at the post of Yamhill, experiencing the usual routine of garrison life without any incidents of much interest, down to the breaking out of the war of the rebellion in April, 1861. The news of the firing on Fort Sumter brought us an excitement which overshadowed all else, and though we had no officers at the post who sympathized with the rebellion, there were several in our regiment—the Fourth Infantry—who did, and we were considerably exercised as to the course they might pursue, but naturally far more so concerning the disposition that would be made of the regiment during the conflict.

In due time orders came for the regiment to go East, and my company went off, leaving me, however—a second lieutenant—in command of the post until I should be relieved by Captain James J. Archer, of the Ninth Infantry, whose company was to take the place of the old garrison. Captain Archer, with his company of the Ninth, arrived shortly after, but I had been notified that he intended to go South, and his conduct was such after reaching the post that I would not turn over the command to him for fear he might commit some rebellious act. Thus a more prolonged detention occurred than I had at first anticipated. Finally the news came that he had tendered his resignation and been granted a leave of absence for sixty days. On July 17 he took his departure, but I continued in command till September 1, when Captain Philip A. Owen, of the Ninth Infantry, arrived and, taking charge, gave me my release.

PHILIP H. SHERIDAN

From the day we received the news of the firing on Sumter until I started East, about the first of September, 1861, I was deeply solicitous as to the course of events, and though I felt confident that in the end the just cause of the Government must triumph, yet the thoroughly crystallized organization which the Southern Confederacy quickly exhibited disquieted me very much, for it alone was evidence that the Southern leaders had long anticipated the struggle and prepared for it. It was very difficult to obtain direct intelligence of the progress of the war. Most of the time we were in the depths of ignorance as to the true condition of affairs, and this tended to increase our anxiety. Then, too, the accounts of the conflicts that had taken place were greatly exaggerated by the Eastern papers, and lost nothing in transition. The news came by the pony express across the Plains to San Francisco, where it was still further magnified in republishing, and gained somewhat in Southern bias. I remember well that when the first reports reached us of the battle of Bull Run—that sanguinary engagement—it was stated that each side had lost *forty* thousand men in killed and wounded, and none were reported missing nor as having run away. Week by week these losses grew less, until they finally shrunk into the hundreds, but the vivid descriptions of the gory conflict were not toned down during the whole summer.

We received our mail at Yamhill only once a week, and then had to bring it from Portland, Oregon, by express. On the day of the week that our courier, or messenger, was expected back from Portland, I would go out early in the morning to a commanding point above the post, from which I could see a long distance down the road as it ran through the valley of the Yamhill, and there I would watch with anxiety for his coming, longing for good news; for, isolated as I had been through years spent in the wilderness, my patriotism was untainted by politics, nor had it been disturbed by any discussion of the questions out of which the war grew, and I hoped for the success of the Government above all other considerations. I believe I was also uninfluenced by any thoughts of the promotion that might result to me from the conflict, but, out of a sincere desire to contribute as much as I could to the preservation of the Union, I earnestly wished to be at the seat of war, and feared it might end before I could get East. In no sense did I anticipate what was to happen to me afterward, nor that I was to gain any distinction from it. I was ready to do my duty to the best of my ability wherever I might be called, and I was young, healthy, insensible to fatigue, and desired opportunity, but high rank was so distant in our service that not a dream of its attainment had flitted through my brain.

During the period running from January to September, 1861, in consequence of resignations and the addition of some new regiments to the regular army, I had passed through the grade of first lieutenant and reached that of captain in the Thirteenth United States Infantry, of which General W.T. Sherman had recently been made the colonel. when relieved from further duty at Yamhill by Captain Owen, I left for the Atlantic coast to join my new regiment. A two days' ride brought me down to Portland, whence I sailed to San Francisco, and at that city took passage by steamer for New York *via* the Isthmus of Panama, in company with a number of officers who were coming East under circumstances like my own.

At this time California was much agitated on the question of secession, and the secession element was so strong that considerable apprehension was felt by the Union people lest the State might be carried into the Confederacy. As a consequence great distrust existed in all quarters, and the loyal passengers on the steamer, not knowing what might occur during our voyage, prepared to meet emergencies by thoroughly organizing to frustrate any attempt that might possibly be made to carry us into some Southern port after we should leave Aspinwall. However, our fears proved groundless; at all events, no such attempt was made, and we reached New York in safety in

November, 1861. A day or two in New York sufficed to replenish a most meagre wardrobe, and I then started West to join my new regiment, stopping a day and a night at the home of my parents in Ohio, where I had not been since I journeyed from Texas for the Pacific coast. The headquarters of my regiment were at Jefferson Barracks, Missouri, to which point I proceeded with no further delay except a stay in the city of St. Louis long enough to pay my respects to General H.W. Halleck.

Index

COLOPHON

The Philip H. Sheridan, INDIAN FIGHTING IN THE FIFTIES IN OREGON AND WASHINGTON TERRITORIES *was printed in the workshop of Glen Adams, which is located in the quiet country village of Fairfield, southern Spokane County in Washington state and one township removed from the Idaho line. Basic book design was by Dale La Tendresse, who also set the book in type, using a Model 7300 Editwriter computer photosetter. The typeface used is 14 on 17 Baskerville with page numbers and running heads in 12 point Baskerville Bold. Camera-darkroom work was by Sylvia Fenich using a 660C DS (Japanese) camera and a LogE automatic film developing machine. The sheets were printed by Dave Hooper using a 28-inch Heidelberg press, model KORS. Folding was by Garry Adams using a 22x28 Baum folding machine. Assembly was by Bonnie Cozzetto. This was a fun project. We had no special difficulty with the work.*

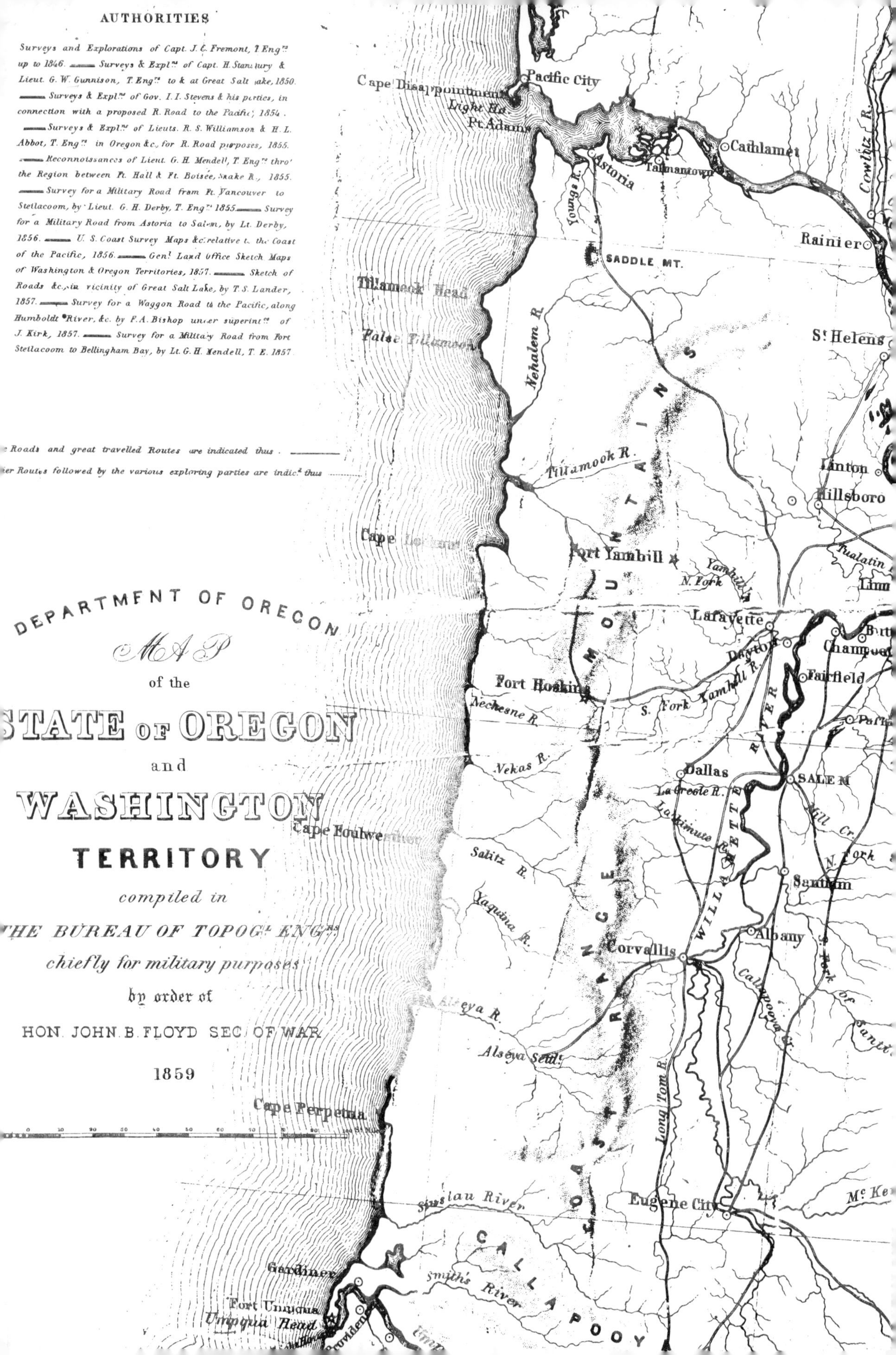

AUTHORITIES

Surveys and Explorations of Capt. J. C. Fremont, T. Eng[rs]. up to 1846. ——— Surveys & Expl[ns] of Capt. H. Stansbury & Lieut. G. W. Gunnison, T. Eng[rs]. to & at Great Salt Lake, 1850. ——— Surveys & Expl[ns] of Gov. I. I. Stevens & his parties, in connection with a proposed R. Road to the Pacific, 1854. ——— Surveys & Expl[ns] of Lieuts. R. S. Williamson & H. L. Abbot, T. Eng[rs]. in Oregon &c., for R. Road purposes, 1855. ——— Reconnoissances of Lieut. G. H. Mendell, T. Eng[rs]. thro' the Region between Ft. Hall & Ft. Boisée, Snake R., 1855. ——— Survey for a Military Road from Ft. Vancouver to Steilacoom, by Lieut. G. H. Derby, T. Eng[rs]. 1855. ——— Survey for a Military Road from Astoria to Salem, by Lt. Derby, 1856. ——— U. S. Coast Survey Maps &c. relative to the Coast of the Pacific, 1856. ——— Genl. Land Office Sketch Maps of Washington & Oregon Territories, 1857. ——— Sketch of Roads &c., in vicinity of Great Salt Lake, by T. S. Lander, 1857. ——— Survey for a Waggon Road to the Pacific, along Humboldt River, &c. by F. A. Bishop under superint[t]. of J. Kirk, 1857. ——— Survey for a Military Road from Fort Steilacoom to Bellingham Bay, by Lt. G. H. Mendell, T. E. 1857.

[e] Roads and great travelled Routes are indicated thus ———
[e]r Routes followed by the various exploring parties are indic[d]. thus ┄┄┄

DEPARTMENT OF OREGON

MAP

of the

STATE OF OREGON

and

WASHINGTON

TERRITORY

compiled in

THE BUREAU OF TOPOG[l]. ENG[rs].

chiefly for military purposes

by order of

HON. JOHN B. FLOYD SEC. OF WAR

1859

0 10 20 30 40 50 60 70 80 90 100 Miles

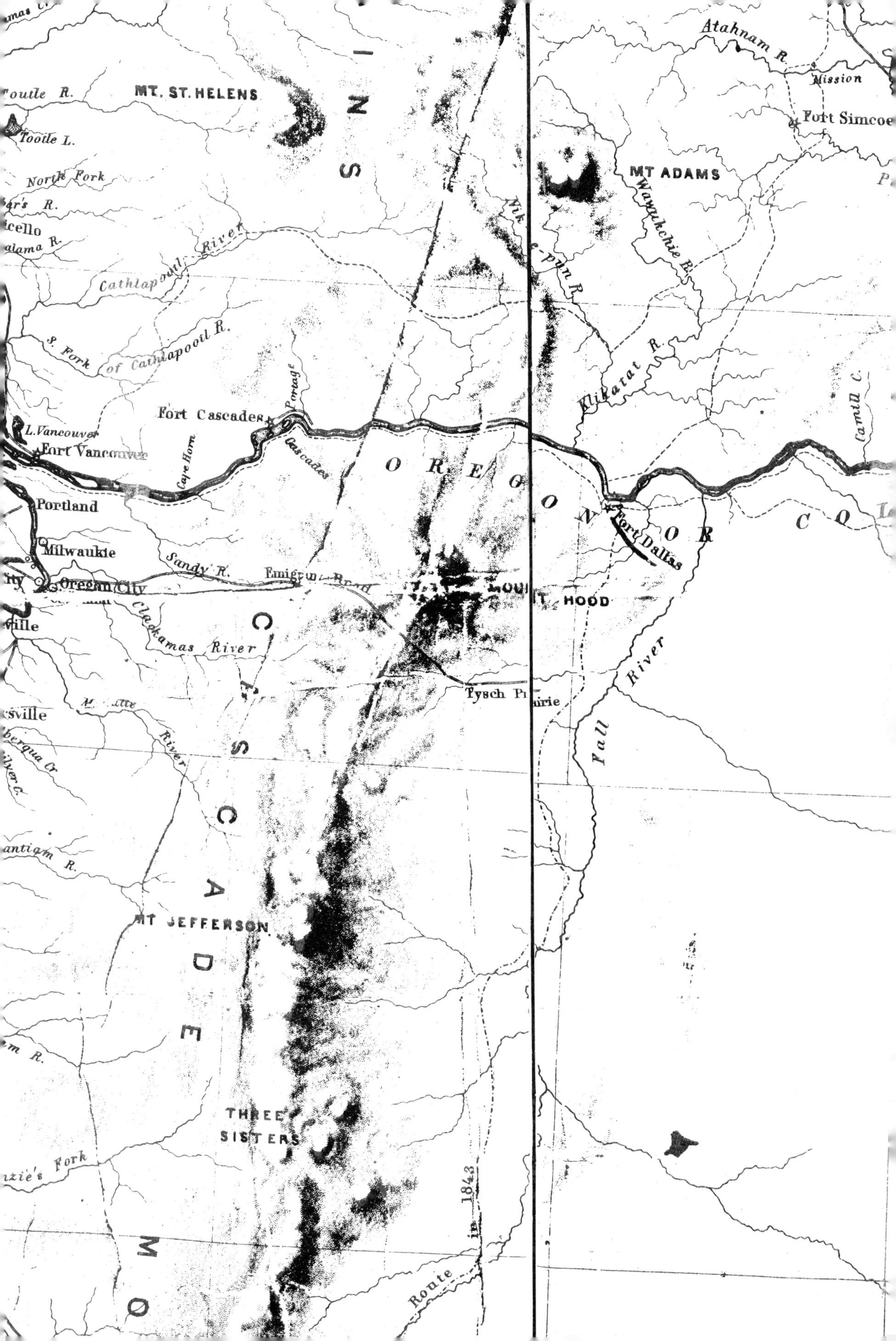

Toutle R.

MT. ST. HELENS

Toutle L.

North Fork

cello

alama R.

Cathlapootl River

Cathlapootl R.

S. Fork of Cathlapootl R.

Fort Cascades

Portage

Cape Horn

Cascades

L. Vancouver

Fort Vancouver

Portland

Milwaukie

Oregon City

ville

Sandy R.

Emigrant Road

Clackamas River

M   tte

River

sville

berqua Cr

River C.

antiam R.

MT JEFFERSON

THREE SISTERS

zie's Fork

MO

CASCADE

OREGON

MOUNT HOOD

Tysch Prairie

Fall River

Route in 1843

MT ADAMS

Nik-e-pun R.

Wawahchie R.

Klikatat R.

Atahnam R.

Mission

Fort Simcoe

Camill C.

Fort Dallas

OR

CO

P